Sacred Geometry

Philosophy & Worldview

D1714942

Scott Onstott

ISBN 979-8744891879

Independently published.

Contents

Introduction

Why I Wrote This Book

I discovered the *sacredness of geometry* many years after working intensively with the more mundane aspects of geometry. First in high school and university, into my early career as architectural draftsman, and then later as a technician specialized in computer-aided design, I worked with quantitative geometry every day. By sketching, measuring, drawing, dimensioning, modeling, and animating, I helped design and visualize numerous complex commercial buildings and their associated mechanical, electrical, and plumbing systems before they were constructed.

After years of working in downtown San Francisco, I eventually made a change from practicing within many large architecture and engineering firms there to teaching students in several Bay Area universities who wanted to follow in my footsteps and build their own careers designing and engineering the built environment.

You never really know something until you teach it to someone else.

John C. Maxwell (1947-), American author and leadership expert

---

It was during my experience teaching over a thousand students in brick-and-mortar classrooms that I discovered geometry also has qualitative aspects, which were initially somewhat mysterious to me and plausibly deniable at first.

Around this time in the late 1990s, I did technical editing of numerous software books and then in the early 2000s I wrote over a dozen of my own technical books and in the 2010s recorded over two dozen video courses on programs such as AutoCAD, Revit, Photoshop, SketchUp, 3ds Max, and Unity. My professional website has links to many of these courses (and much more of my activity besides):

www.scott.training

All through this process of focusing on geometry through design software, I experienced numerous occasions where I had to come up with sample projects to demonstrate various program features. As an admirer of great design, I gave myself time and space to draw for the sake of drawing, ostensibly to come up with compelling design projects for my courses.

In this spirit I started drawing crop circle geometry around the turn of the millennium—just for the fun of it. I set aside the issue of who makes crop circles, because it really should primarily be all about the amazing geometry in my view. It is always a challenge to interpret the internal logic of any complex geometry when your references can only be aerial perspective photos of crops selectively laid flat in the fields.

Through this practice of drawing for the sake of drawing, manually with pencil, ruler & compass on paper and far more accurately with AutoCAD, I undeniably experienced the *preciousness* or *sacredness of geometry.* I did not share my experience with anyone about how much fun I was having with crop circle geometry because at the time I thought it would make me seem crazy. This is probably due to the massive blind spot the dominant paradigm has even for the possibility of a genuine phenomenon, so large you can fly a ball of light right through it—but that is another story.

In 2009 I was open enough from my experiences with crop circle geometry to seek guidance from unusual consultant Marcia Schafer on my direction in life.

She told me that I was about to make a film. I was incredulous, never having made any type of videos other than software tutorials! She said making the film would be an important milestone in my personal journey, but what it was going to be about she did not say— that was for me to figure out.

Believe it or not, I took her little psychic nudge very seriously indeed, and it took me a full year to write, narrate, and produce an online documentary series running over 5 hours long in two volumes called "Secrets in Plain Sight." It premiered on YouTube in 2010 and since then many millions of people have watched the series. You can still rent both volumes ad-free on my website or watch volume 1 if you are a subscriber on:

gaia.com

Secrets in Plain Sight reveals many patterns in art, architecture, urban design & in the cosmos that are right there but previously went largely unperceived. Making people conscious of these sometimes-uncanny patterns in the world has made a lasting impact, and I have received tons of positive feedback and even some testimonials from people who say their lives and outlooks have been changed forever.

I originally met Geoff Fitzpatrick, who is now my co-host at Sacred Geometry Academy, expressly because he watched my documentary series and felt inspired to interview me for his website:

mandalanature.com

In the interview Geoff asked me the very question which inspired him to request the interview, "Have you ever studied crop circles?" It seemed to him such an obvious oversight to not be included in my series that he yearned to fill me in on the phenomenon and its amazing geometric patterns.

I explained to Geoff that I saw crop circles as the very catalyst that resulted in my series and I am amazed that is what also brought us together. I explained that when I wrote the series in 2010, I felt that crop circles were just too controversial a subject. I avoided mentioning them—something I now regret given cultural developments in the intervening years.

Geoff and I went on to become friends online and offline. Given our mutual love of geometry, we eventually co-hosted weekend workshops at the Transpersonal Institute in County Meath, Ireland for two years running. After the pandemic we plan to resume residential workshops like these, which are fantastic experiences.

The 2010s saw a massive rise in mythologic thinking, including illuminati and reptilian elite conspiracy theorists, flat-Earth truthers, and the rise of belief in Q anon conspiracies. I do not have the inclination or the interest to pursue any of the listed theories in any shape or form.

Even though I steered away from covering crop circles, which I adore but considered too loaded a topic, the rational but outside-the-box thinking of my *Secrets in Plain Sight* documentary series attracted what I perceived as much unwanted attention from many fanatical adherents of disorganized systems of belief. In retrospect, crop circles are not conspiracies, and qualitatively quite different. You do not have to believe anything to verify that crop circles are real or to appreciate their geometries.

Explaining their authorship is where things can get contentious, but that issue is really beside the point that the anonymous authors are making every year—which must be the geometry in itself!

The quantitative experience of geometry has been used for thousands of years as the means to teach logical thinking and rationality, something members of both organized and disorganized systems of belief would do well to study.

The qualitative experience of geometry and its palpable *sacredness* is something I knew in my very being but struggled for years to cognitively understand on my own, much less become skilled to pass on to others. While my 36 years of practice (starting with high school drafting) continues to unfold, little did I know that my mind was being quietly upgraded by my persistent fascination with geometry.

Man's mind, once stretched by a new idea, never regains its original dimensions.

Oliver Wendell Holmes, Jr (1841-1935), one of the most widely cited United States Supreme Court justices in history, known for his concise opinions.

It took decades of life experience, with loads of drawing, reading, watching, contemplating, and teaching for me to articulate my experiences as a complete philosophy and self-consistent worldview, which resulted in *a different way of thinking about everything.*

I find this way incredibly positive, healing and verifiably transformative. This book is my attempt to share my philosophy & worldview for your consideration and cognitive appreciation, should you decide to embark on this journey yourself or are trying to make sense of your own after previously experiencing the *sacredness of geometry.*

What this Book IS NOT

Not About Drawing

This book does not discuss drawing techniques or how to draw to experience qualitative geometry yourself. That is the purpose of this book's companion courses, which feature pre-recorded videos, and live face-to-face interaction with the author, co-host, and other course participants. Please visit:

sacredgeometryacademy.com

...for more information about how you can enroll in a free mini course to see what it is all about, and to optionally continue with the experience in the full paid course.

Not Another Belief System

The philosophy presented here is not meant to become yet another belief system to have faith in, but rather a worldview that you can rationally evaluate and contemplate. It is entirely up to you to decide if the worldview presented in this book explains your experience better than the dominant paradigm.

It is the mark of an educated mind to be able to entertain a thought without accepting it.

Aristotle (384-322 BC), Plato's famous student who focused on empirical research, was the first to study biology systematically. Aristotle was interested in studying geology, astronomy, philosophy, psychology, economics, politics, ethics and much more.

Ask questions, refine, and improve upon my ideas if you feel inspired to do so. This is not a gospel or "download" from on high, but a rational work in progress.

I don't have to have faith, I have experience.

Joseph Campbell (1904-1987) was an American professor of literature who worked in comparative mythology and comparative religion.

The ideas in this book do not subscribe to the dominant paradigm of materialism/physicalism or any organized system of belief (religion) or disorganized system of belief (conspiracy theories). It is not scientism, or creationism, intelligent design by a deity or deities, or a new religion in disguise.

Some are uncomfortable with ideas which do not fit comfortably within the dominant paradigm. If you can tolerate these ideas, more power to you. However, I caution against trying to convince people of ideas because you see the wisdom in them, or simply because they are novel ideas. It is healthy to be able to take different perspectives.

I learned through my experience in creating Secrets in Plain Sight, that it is best not to push ideas on others. Just offering them to people who seek them out is enough. Sometimes people will not be remotely interested. Perhaps they will be someday or perhaps never—either way, that is their business, and it is best to respect others.

However, any honest recommendation or testimonial about how the ideas in this book or how the qualitative experience with geometry in my course has transformed you is very much appreciated. I know that those seeking this type of information will probably love this book, just as I do. If you are one of these people, then this book was literally written for you.

Not Enough in Itself

This is meant to be a companion to my course and aid to personal transformation. Philosophy may be remarkably interesting and especially helpful for understanding, but an abiding left-brained love of knowledge is not typically enough to transform your whole being to an entirely new worldview, probably because we are extraordinarily complex, and it takes time and practice for anything to really sink in. However, the information in this book may give you a clearer cognitive picture of why the *sacredness of geometry* can transform a person's whole outlook and how anyone can engage in that practice should they wish to.

This book is a companion to my courses which offer direct first-hand experiences with qualitative geometry, where we engage multiple core drives such as the quest for meaning, exploring states of consciousness without brain altering chemicals, expressing yourself creatively, and communing face-to-face in private groups.

This book can be digested either before or after taking courses in Sacred Geometry Academy. If you read it before, it will likely pique your interest in what follows and if you read it after, it will put your experiences in a context that may help you to understand them more fully—very satisfying in my experience.

Not for Academia

I did not write this in an academic dialect but in the common tongue for you, dear seeker. I am not a professional philosopher so please forgive my naïveté. The content of the world's libraries is now at our fingertips, and academia no longer has the monopoly on ideas it once did.

I am a co-founder of the Sacred Geometry Academy website, which for now is run by two persons with a shared vision to reinterpret Plato's famous Academy for the current time.

What This Book IS

It is Meta

It is about the whole body experiencing *the sacredness of geometry* but as a book or eBook, it is necessarily on the level of mental abstraction. This does not guide you through the qualitative experience of sacred geometry but attempts to unpack what that experience implies.

It is Interspersed with Great Thinkers Aphorisms

My recommendation is for you to be generous in giving yourself a bit of time and space to read, re-read and contemplate each quote in this book. They are not just table dressings. Great thinkers' aphorisms are delicacies, rolling lifetimes of wisdom into easily digestible, bite-sized morsels of wisdom. My intention in including quotes is not for you to paste them on stock photos and turn them into memes on Twitter. Instead, these quotes are not platitudes but powerful ideas that have been strategically selected to catalyze your understanding of my exposition.

The safest general characterization of the European philosophical tradition is that it consists of a series of footnotes to Plato.

Alfred North Whitehead (1861-1947) was an English philosopher and mathematician. He wrote the Principia Mathematica with Bertrand Russell, one of the 20th century's most important works in the logic of mathematics.

It is Classified as Idealism

My philosophy is classified as an idealist post-modern reinterpretation of the Platonic tradition which integrates the spiritual teachings of non-dualism, transpersonal psychology, and a new theory of mind.

It is an Alternative Worldview

An alternative way of thinking is spelled out in Part II, complete with its own ontology (study of being), epistemology (study of knowing), and teleology (study of causes), which together attempt to make sense of experiencing *the sacredness of geometry.*

Part I: The Marvel of Geometry

1 | Quick Geometric Primer

Geometry can be considered from at least three viewpoints.
First as a technical exercise mostly serving industrialization.
Secondly as a purely mathematical function. Thirdly, and
most importantly, as a science of the soul. This has to be
performed with the human hand and is fundamental to a
deeper understanding of the Platonic wisdom tradition.
Geometry is only fully understood by doing it.

*Keith Critchlow (1933-2020) was an artist, professor of architecture, and
a co-founder of the Temenos Academy. He wrote many excellent books on
sacred geometry and was a personal hero of the author.*

Quantitative Uses of Geometry

This branch is geometry's most popular one and is by far its
most practical. Using geometry to draft, design, dimension, and
model forms—or to measure the world—is essential in countless
technical professions such as architecture, engineering, industrial
design, electronic circuit design, many disciplines of science and
even in entertainment in terms of set design, increasingly in
animations and special effects and even in stock market and crypto
investment.

As to the usefulness of geometry, it is as certain that no curious art or mechanic work can either be invented, improved, or performed without its assisting principles.

Benjamin Franklin (1706-1790) was a polymath and 'founding father' of the United States of America.

My career started with manual drafting in the 1980s, and I was a huge proponent of the tectonic shift which transformed numerous analog professions to using digital tools. In the process we gained tremendous practical advantages and can now quantify, design, simulate, and build things today that were never possible previously. It was a marvelous revolution.

However, I can tell you that in the process we also lost something essential—the visceral linkage between hand, paper, and world that drawing with the human body used to bring to the table.

Consider for a moment that people experienced this natural connection from the origin of civilization until the early 1990s. Those whose careers started later are probably intellectually aware of the tectonic shift in technology, but fewer still are viscerally aware of the sensibility of stylus, ruler, and compass and what that natural immediacy meant to countless generations.

Understanding how to use geometry quantitatively can help you get a job or improve your professional skills. Most of my career focused on learning, using, and teaching AutoCAD (and other design software) to members of the Architecture—Engineering—Construction industry.

The quantitative use of geometry can fulfill the core human desire to learn, build skills, work, achieve, and succeed in many industries.

Mathematical Uses of Geometry

Geometry's mathematical use is abstract and markedly different from its quantitative use, which is concerned more with practical matters. The mathematical use of geometry includes within itself an inner logic that was spotted early in the history of civilization. Euclid lived in Alexandria and was likely born around 325 BC, but we sadly do not know more than this one fact about his life. I speculate that Euclid was less the discoverer of geometric theorems himself and more a brilliant chronicler of the common mathematical knowledge of his contemporaries, who were themselves informed by knowledge passed down from Egyptians, Sumerians, and other civilizations ancient even in Euclid's time. However, that is beside the point—Euclid is identified the author of <u>The Elements</u>[1], he was Greek, and that is enough.

I do not think people appreciate just how influential the mathematical uses of geometry have been in the development of rationality. Euclid's Elements was the most popular textbook ever published and was required reading up until the early 20th century.

It is sometimes said that next to the Bible, Euclid's The Elements may be the most translated, published, and studied of all the books produced in the Western world.

Bartel Leendert van der Waerden (1903-1996), historian of mathematics.

Many have been subjected to the "mathematical use" in their geometry class during secondary education (high school), but sadly most saw this as a form of unusually cruel punishment. Do not worry—that is not what this book is about.

---

[1] https://bit.ly/3rQ0EC7

Geometry and mathematical education in general have been falling short for a long time. In 2011 one survey found, "77% of the students seemed to believe that math was not something that could be figured out, or that made sense. It was just a set of procedures and rules to be memorized. This is, of course, exactly the opposite of true."[2]

Given the failure of stimulating conceptual thinking in students, it is no wonder pre-rational mythic belief has erupted onto the global stage. Democracy is itself a rational creation which requires at least that stage of cognition within its citizens to function effectively.

Euclid showed how geometry can teach us to think clearly. From a few simple axioms, an entire interconnected edifice of logic can be reconstructed in each mind.

Abraham Lincoln studied and nearly mastered the Six-books of Euclid (geometry) since he was a member of Congress. He began a course of rigid mental discipline with the intent to improve his faculties, especially his powers of logic and language. Hence his fondness for Euclid, which he carried with him on the circuit till he could demonstrate with ease all the propositions in the six books; often studying far into the night, with a candle near his pillow, while his fellow-lawyers, half a dozen in a room, filled the air with interminable snoring.

William Herndon (1818-1891), law partner and biographer of Abraham Lincoln

---

[2] https://bit.ly/3vrpkmv

Please consider carefully what a few brilliant minds well acquainted with geometry's mathematical use wrote about their experience...

Geometry is the rules of all mental investigation.

Mikhail Lomonosov (1711-1756) was a polymath, scientist, and writer, who made important contributions to literature, education, and science.

It is marvelous enough that man is capable at all to reach such a degree of certainty and purity in pure thinking as the Greeks showed us for the first time to be possible in geometry.

Albert Einstein (1879-1955) is widely acknowledged to be one of the greatest physicists of all time.

Equations are just the boring part of mathematics. I attempt to see things in terms of geometry.

Stephen Hawking (1942-2018) was the first to set out a theory of cosmology explained by a union of the general theory of relativity and quantum mechanics.

Qualitative Uses of Geometry

It is only from this least popular viewpoint of quality that we can perceive geometry's *precious* or *sacred* quality. Critchlow described this as something having "to be performed with the human hand" to be fully understood, and that is precisely what the curated experience offers in this book's companion course.

Geometry's qualitative use does not require or impart rationality as does geometry's mathematical use, and the qualitative has none of the practical applications that geometry's quantitative use does. So, what does "qualitative" even mean? *Qualitative* as a word is used most often in contrast with *quantitative*. Qualitative is an adjective that describes the noun *quality*, which is in turn defined as "the character or nature of something." Where is the character or nature of something defined? This is not defined anywhere. We must turn to philosophy to find a hint.

In philosophy, *quale* (singular) or *qualia* (plural) is defined as "a quality as perceived or experienced by a person." So, must we now ask a person about the subjective qualia they experience? Exactly.

The qualitative use of geometry points to the experiencing subject beyond language who understands its meaning. Only consciousness can experience what geometry is like. We experience the taste of chocolate, the color of a sunset, or the qualia of geometry but only consciousness understands what each experience means. We may not be able to articulate each meaning, but we know them. We might best describe each above quale as being simply good, beautiful, or true, respectively. All conscious beings know what good, beautiful, and true experiences are when we experience them—they are the best. So too is the qualitative use of geometry!

Qualia are precisely what differentiate self-conscious beings from machines, the experience of *what it is like*. In any case, qualia and consciousness are inextricably entangled. That must be why Critchlow called this use of geometry the "science of the soul."

I think it will be helpful if, before diving into the next chapter, you experience the qualia of what a few great minds across the ages had to say about geometry, which I have listed here in chronological order.

Antiquity

Geometry is knowledge of the eternally existent. -Pythagoras

Mighty is geometry; joined with art, irresistible. -Euripides

It is through geometry that one purifies the eye of the soul. -Plato

Geometry is the art of the eternally true. -Socrates

Medieval

Geometry enlightens the intellect and sets one's mind right. All its proofs are very clear and orderly. It is hardly possible for errors to enter into geometrical reasoning, because it is well arranged and orderly. Thus, the mind that constantly applies itself to geometry is not likely to fall into error. In this convenient way, the person who knows geometry acquires intelligence. -Ibn Khaldun

Renaissance

Let no one who is not a mathematician read my works. -Leonardo da Vinci

Without mathematics there is no art."-Luca Pacioli

Since geometry is the right foundation of all painting, I have decided to teach its rudiments and principles to all youngsters eager for art. -Albrecht Dürer

Many arts there are which beautify the mind of man; but of all none do more garnish and beautify it than those arts which are called mathematical, unto the knowledge of which no man can attain, without perfect knowledge and instruction of the principles, grounds, and Elements of Geometry. -John Dee

Enlightenment

Geometry is the archetype of the beauty of the world. -Johannes Kepler

Geometry is the only science that it hath pleased God hitherto to bestow on mankind. -Thomas Hobbes

It is the glory of geometry that from so few principles, fetched from without, it is able to accomplish so much. -Isaac Newton

A work of morality, politics, criticism will be more elegant, other things being equal, if it is shaped by the hand of geometry. -Bernard le Bovier de Fontenelle

Modern

Geometry, to which I have devoted my life, is honoured with the title of the Key of Sciences. -Benjamin Peirce

I have come to realize that each expression of sentiment is made by a movement governed by geometry. Geometry is everywhere present in nature. A woman combing her hair goes through a series of rhythmic movements that constitute a beautiful harmony. The entire rhythm of the body is governed by geometric law. -François Auguste Rene Rodin

Geometry is knowledge that appears to be produced by human beings, yet whose meaning is totally independent of them. -Rudolf Steiner

2 | Unpacking Sacredness

Explaining why the qualitative use of geometry can be experienced in consciousness as a transpersonal, palpably *sacred experience*—completely independently of the baggage of religious or spiritual traditions—is the aim of this chapter.

I have arranged the following sections in a logical, linear order to take you step-by-step to the next level of thinking about geometry.

Conscious Experience

This book cannot give you the feeling of the exquisiteness, preciousness, trueness, or sacredness of geometry. These are qualia which must be "performed by the human hand" and directly experienced. This book presupposes that primary felt experience and unpacks what its palpable quality implies.

Universal Mathematics & Geometry

Geometry is the extension of number in space. As such, it is classified as a subset of mathematics, which in essence is the study of symbolic relationships between numbers. Remarkably, people have been doing mathematics as far back as written records exist.

Like many fields of study, mathematics is divided into numerous branches or topics which focus in on aspects of the subject. These include but are by no means limited to basic/advanced, pure/applied, algebra, calculus, geometry, combinatorics, logic, number theory, differential equations, vector calculus, and so on. Geometry itself has its own sub-branches, of which Euclidean, non-Euclidean, Riemannian, Complex, are just a few.

All these branches, subdivisions, and topics are made for epistemic (practical) reasons, not ontic (real) ones.

> One geometry cannot be more true than another; it can only be more convenient.

Henri Poincaré (1854-1912), known as 'The Last Universalist', was a polymath mathematician, theoretical physicist, engineer, and philosopher of science.

Although we use different symbols and words to describe mathematical and geometric concepts, the reality they reference remains universally the same throughout human history.

There is no specific American, Chinese, or Scythian geometry, belonging only to specific cultures across time. The fascinating history of science is certainly attributable to individuals and describes their contributions. The contributors were and are embedded in specific cultures, but geometry itself contains no such relative qualifiers or "baggage."

Geometry & mathematical formulae are specially exempted from ever being patentable worldwide. No one can claim a pure geometric form or any mathematical formula as their proprietary creation. For example, triangles and $E=mc^2$ will always be in the public domain.

Mathematics is like a Gothic cathedral that one can enter through any of its three doors and consciously explore the inner architecture indefinitely. These doors include Geometry (number extended in space), Music (number extended in time) and the Philosophy of Universals. The edifice of mathematics was there long before human minds and will still be there long after all we humans are gone.

Numbers existed before the objects described by them.

Plotinus (204-270) was a Neoplatonist philosopher who lived in Roman Egypt. He is best known for writing the <u>Enneads</u>.

Geometry existed before the creation. It is co-eternal with the mind of God.

Johannes Kepler (1571-1630) was a key figure in the scientific revolution, best known for his three laws of planetary motion.

If we ever meet extra-terrestrials which are truly alien to us—not just humanoid English speakers with cosmetically different ears or noses—our best hope lies in using either geometry or music to establish meaningful communication.

Mathematics is pure language, the language of science.

Alfred Adler (1870-1937) was a medical doctor, psychotherapist, and founder of the school of individual psychology.

Speaking of universal languages, one that did not work out was Esperanto, a 19th century attempt at a "constructed international second language." As it turned out, the attempt was criticized as being highly Eurocentric, inherently sexist, and never took off as its creator had hoped. So much for creating universality.

Mathematics has always been, is, and shall eternally be the "universal language" not just on this planet, but presumably everywhere in the universe.

Languages are Maps

All languages are maps, and not the territories they describe. I will try and explain through a few essential theorems of logic and informal reasoning.

Gödel's Incompleteness Theorems

In 1930 Kurt Gödel delivered his incompleteness theorems, which essentially proved two things. Informally they are:

1. If an axiomatic formal system is consistent, it cannot be complete.
2. Consistency of axioms cannot be proven within their own system.

Those two statements sound straightforward, but with them Gödel proved that axiomatic formal systems (aka mathematics) are either consistent but incomplete, or complete but inconsistent.

Mathematics is nothing if not consistent, so Gödel essentially proved that mathematics itself will forever be fundamentally incomplete.

Gödel's mind operated on a logical level far above everyone else. He was one of the most significant logicians in history.

Kurt Gödel's achievement in modern logic is singular and monumental—indeed it is more than a monument, it is a landmark which will remain visible far in space and time. The subject of logic has certainly completely changed its nature and possibilities with Gödel's achievement.

John von Neumann (1903-1957), the foremost mathematician of his time, integrated pure and applied sciences.

Tarksi's Undefinability Theorem

In 1933, just two years after Gödel dropped the L-bomb, Alfred Tarski, another on the short list of greatest logicians of all time, published his undefinability theorem, which is related in how it defines limits to the foundations of mathematics and formal semantics (the study of meaning).

Informally, Tarski's theorem states that *arithmetical truth cannot be defined in arithmetic*. It also shows that *language cannot represent its own semantics*. In simpler terms:

1. Language does not contain meaning.
2. Meaning exists outside language, only in consciousness.

An anecdote might help you to understand the undefinability theorem. Imagine when you were a small child and your parent pointed to an apple and either said and/or wrote "apple, pomme, manzana, قط ،مدينة ،تفاحة, 苹果," or something similar.

You associated the fruit with sounds and/or letters. Meaning does not exist within the language, which consists only of sounds or symbols that stand as cultural referents, but the meaning of any language is universally understood only by consciousness.

It follows that languages do not suddenly spring out of nowhere, they must be expressly created by consciousness—just as mariners make maps to chart the seas they sail, so they know where they are in the territory.

You are the Territory

If math is the universal language, and is also fundamentally incomplete (Gödel), what must math be missing? Math is necessarily missing meaning, which cannot be represented within any language (Tarski).

This is what I mean when I stated at the outset that languages are maps and not the territories they describe. The territory of the universal language is consciousness—you who understand meaning. You understand what "1+1=2" means and what a "triangle" is. You are the territory, but relative minds are only capable of using maps that point to the absolute, real you.

Incidentally, if meaning cannot be consistently and completely defined in any language, mind, or listed by algorithm, then this has implications for computing machines that we build to perform algorithmic computations.

Algorithmic classical computers will never be conscious like we are. They will remain maps—mere "artificial intelligence" machines.

Let us pretend that there was a machine, which was constructed in such a way as to give rise to thinking, sensing, and having perceptions. You could imagine it expanded in size (while retaining the same proportions) so that you could go inside it, like going into a mill. On this assumption, your tour inside it would show you the working parts pushing each other, but never anything which would explain a perception.

Gottfried Wilhelm von Leibnitz (1646-1716) was one of the most important logicians, mathematicians, and natural philosophers of the Enlightenment. He developed calculus at the same time as Isaac Newton.

I speculate that quantum computers may possibly one day exhibit signs of conscious general intelligence, but only if it turns out that systematic quantum indeterminacy is identified within the neurons of the human brain. If so, our brains are quantum computers. If not, then there is a subtle connection to a realm outside the system of the world which we have yet to discover, which "would explain a perception," as Leibnitz put it so well.

Neither World Nor Individual Mind

There is no such thing as a point (0D), line (1D), square (2D), cube (3D), tesseract (4D) or any other such ideal form in the material world, no matter how many or how few dimensions it occupies in the mind.

A line is length without breadth.

Euclid (325 BC - mid 3rd century BC), is known as the father of geometry.

Zooming in with a microscope on a straight pencil line drawn on a sheet of paper is to see a craggy streak of graphite smeared across a landscape of cellulose.

No matter how precisely constructed, pure geometry cannot exist within a matrix of atoms consisting of spatial units which ultimately exhibit granularity at small scale. Drawing a line in the world is only a rough approximation of an ideal line at best.

Consider the following analogy of Photoshop & Illustrator (both programs made by Adobe, Inc). Pictures in Photoshop are primarily represented by modulating a raster array of pixels, frozen in a specific resolution like things made from atoms. Designs in Illustrator are primarily vector shapes driven by pure mathematical equations, which make them independent of the picture's resolution. Geometry is independent of the world as vector shapes are independent of the resolution of raster images.

Numbers and geometry simply do not exist in the world as material objects. We may count apples on our fingertips, but this is conscious association, rather than material identity. We understand the meaning of the count and can abstract the math from the material and perform mathematical operations on the numbers (adding, subtracting, etc.) to serve the practical needs of inventory in the world and of commerce. However, geometry and number are not in the world.

We could present spatially an atomic fact which contradicted the laws of physics, but not one which contradicted the laws of geometry.

Ludwig Wittgenstein (1889-1951) worked primarily in logic and the philosophies of mathematics, mind, and language.

Geometry and math are not relative to the perspective of an individual mind, nor the cultural context in which they are assessed. In other words, geometry and math are a special or pure form of truth which is absolute.

Another Domain

If geometry does not exist in the material world and remains independently true in all conceivable times, places, and cultures, then where does it exist?

We must necessarily posit another domain beyond the material world to explain the intelligibility of mathematics and geometry. How else can we explain that we understand mathematics and geometry—even if some understand more than others? There must be some domain of reference that all who understand a concept as simple as *triangle* all are universally accessing.

There exists another domain which is populated by geometry and mathematical entities, which are non-spatial and non-temporal, immaterial in nature. Amazingly, consciousness has the capability of accessing this universally intelligible domain.

Each of us can manifest the properties of a field of consciousness that transcends space, time, and linear causality.

Stanislav Grof (1931-) is one of the principal developers of transpersonal psychology and research into the use of non-ordinary states of consciousness for purposes of exploring, healing, and obtaining growth and insights into the human psyche.

I will detail the qualities of this domain and others in the epistemology of Part II. For now, it is enough to contemplate why this domain must inescapably exist, and that we can access it universally through consciousness.

3 | Collision with the Dominant Paradigm

In the previous section I claimed that another domain populated by geometry and mathematical entities exists in my epistemology.

Okay Houston, we've had a problem here.

NASA Apollo 13 spaceflight (1970)

We tend to operate with many unexamined assumptions in the dominant paradigm under which we all live, in every nation on planet Earth today. The givens listed in this section are part of what I characterize as the *standard worldview*, named so to differentiate them from the *alternative worldview* described in Part II. Let us now become aware of some of the false assumptions within the standard worldview.

The Universe is Independent of Consciousness

Until recently physicists assumed that the universe was made entirely of matter and energy (plus the laws of physics which govern their interactions). Then *dark* matter and *dark* energy were postulated to account for measured discrepancies with accepted theories of gravity. Alarmingly, these dark discrepancies add up to 95% of the total mass-energy content of the universe.

Worse still, neither dark matter nor dark energy have been directly observed, and may never be detectible, not even in principle, because dark matter and energy do not (or possibly only very weakly interact) with newly renamed *ordinary* mass and *ordinary* energy through gravity. Okay, Houston, we really have a problem now.

If the universe is made from any combination of ordinary or dark mass-energy that makes the math work out with gravity, where does that math—and, for that matter, all the laws of physics which govern the continuing interaction of the total mass-energy—reside? These laws are immaterial ideas, which are not made of the material-energetic stuff of the universe. In whose mind do all these abstractions and ideas reside?

The laws of physics must not reside only in human minds because mathematics is the only language valid everywhere in the universe and its laws govern the interactions of the total mass-energy of the universe—which they have done long before humans arrived in a tiny corner of the universe quite recently—and presumably these same laws will continue to apply long into the post-human future.

As with all languages, meaning and semantic understanding logically reside outside them. How is it then that we can consciously understand at least some of the universal language, being made entirely (albeit from only an infinitesimal portion) of the total mass-energy of the universe? Where does that understanding of mathematics reside?

The belief that any such abstractions such as the laws of physics, ordinary matter, ordinary energy, dark matter, and dark energy exist independently of consciousness is precisely that—an abstract belief—not an observation anyone (not even the universal mind) can ever experience. How can laws which can be understood only by consciousness govern a universe which exists independently of consciousness? This entire assumption is clearly a false belief.

Consciousness is a Hard Problem

Although consciousness is admittedly a "hard problem"[1] to explain, the assumption is that it must somehow "emerge" as an epiphenomenon within brain tissue, because after all, that is what we experience from the first-person perspective. With more imaging and research into the brain's inner workings we assume that one day scientists might discover what gives rise to our vital experience of consciousness.

However, consciousness cannot arise from any possible configuration of stuff outside itself, even in principle. Consciousness is not just a hard problem—it is an outright impossibility if you believe that consciousness emerges from brains made of unconscious matter.

I regard consciousness as fundamental. I regard matter as derivative from consciousness. We cannot get behind consciousness. Everything we talk about, everything that we regard as existing, postulates consciousness.

Max Planck (1858-1947), his discovery of energy quanta (as originator of quantum theory) won him the Nobel Prize in Physics in 1918.

So deeply taken with the assumptions of the standard worldview, some believe consciousness is an illusion created by their brains—this is the philosophy within eliminative materialism called illusionism.[2]

---

[1] Chalmers, David (2003). Consciousness and its Place in Nature
[2] https://en.wikipedia.org/wiki/Eliminative_materialism#Illusionism

The problem with the illusionism stance is not about denying consciousness as a third-person object which we study in brains, but that it fails to account for our own first-person conscious experience. You will doubtless agree that you know the phenomenon of experiencing—including experiencing illusions—better than anything, or are you not alive?

You Only Have One Life to Live

This assumption is based on the observation that when a person's brain activity ceases their consciousness also appears to end—at which point they typically die. Brain death is used as an indicator of legal death in many jurisdictions.

In rare cases of medically induced comas and other accidental near-death experiences, some subjects have later reported rich phenomenal experiences which occurred during periods when their brains measured no activity whatsoever.[3]

There is a rich literature about the phenomenology of near-death and out-of-body experiences which proceed through a series of identical transpersonal stages, verified by many people's conscious experience.

Research on reincarnation[4] and altered states of consciousness[5] show, at minimum, that there is much more to reality than the material body.

To assume that we only have one life to live, we must necessarily ignore or dismiss at least all the following realms of experience:

- Testimony of those who revived from near-death experiences.

---

[3] Alexander, Eben (2012) Proof of Heaven: A Neurosurgeon's Journey into the Afterlife

[4] Stevenson, Ian (1988) Children Who Remember Previous Lives: A Question of Reincarnation

[5] Bache, Christopher (2017) LSD and the Mind of the Universe: Diamonds from Heaven

- Reincarnation, the phenomenon of pre-existing immaterial souls being born into new material bodies.
- Communication with souls of the deceased not yet reincarnated through mediums.
- Thousands of years of accumulated wisdom from nearly every religion and spiritual tradition, which typically have a lot to say about consciousness continuing after death.
- Altered states of consciousness in which people experience phenomenal reality outside the physical body.

Only after comprehensive denial of the above bulleted points can we legitimately assume we only have one life to live. Remarkably, people mostly do precisely this, all without much reflection. We probably do this because of deeply ingrained assumptions built into the standard worldview.

None of these points can be scientifically proven because stories cannot be weighed or measured as they rely entirely on conscious testimony, which the standard worldview already assumes arises in the brain—so these must be collective hallucinations or the products of over-active belief systems.

It is impossible for a man to learn what he thinks he already knows.

Epictetus (50-135) was a Greek stoic philosopher. He taught that philosophy is not only theoretical, but a way of life.

What if, for example, reincarnation is real? If your individuality somehow could survive the death of your body—would that cause you live this life any differently? Would you still fear death in the same way?

Everything is Relative

Claiming "everything is relative" is a performative contradiction because it contradicts its own implicit assumption of being absolutely true. Those embracing the standard worldview have been under this false assumption, ever since post-modernism took over the intellectual life of universities in the second half of the 20th century. Not everything is relative—but cultures and societies emphatically are. We can see that easily by comparing them.

The philosophy of post-modernism which developed in France in the mid-20th century was instrumental in revealing truths which are relative to the historical, social, and cultural contexts in which they are embedded, and in deconstructing how power and ideology continue to inform commonly held beliefs.

Where this attitude goes too far is when it acts with absolute privilege in deconstructing everything in the name of relativism. It becomes toxic when denying the very existence of truth, goodness, beauty, and logic, which if true would tear down even its own comprehension.

If we apply the philosophy of relativism to itself, we then perceive post-modernism within its historical context as a 20th century thesis against the values of modernism which grew out of the 18th century Enlightenment, whose implicit absolutism is the very antithesis of relativism. Now in the 21st century, the time is ripe for a synthesis combining the best of both philosophies while simultaneously transcending them with something new.

In this synthesis, I perceive there is now space to integrate both transcendent conceptions of truth, goodness, beauty & logic, along with immanent conceptions of the same, which are embedded in specific historical, sociocultural contexts.

Meaning is Irrelevant

If we assume everything is relative, then whatever universal truths anyone asserts can be deconstructed and shown to be belief systems (aka comforting illusions), which are relative products of the originating sociocultural contexts.

Even after post-modern intellectuals deconstruct relative, partial truths, people are still going to believe whatever they want to believe. Whatever meaning people ascribe to their own reality is ultimately their individual business.

Therefore, the stance is that we essentially no longer need care about what people find meaningful, because tracking online behaviors and geolocating movements (aka "big data") is a far more efficient predictor and shaper of future buying habits and life patterns—highly profitable data for commerce and law enforcement.

The standard worldview's underlying assumption that *meaning is irrelevant* described above negates the irrepressible natural quest for meaning that all psyches share. The core drive for meaning stimulates people to look for it in organized systems of belief, disorganized systems of belief, by believing only in oneself, trying to find transpersonal meaning on one's own, or not believing in anything at all. In other words, we often find meaning within religion, conspiracy theories, narcissism, the process of seeking, nihilism, and possibly in many other ways.

We are all here on earth to help others; what on earth the others are here for I don't know.

W. H. Auden (1907-1973) was an American poet.

What is the meaning of life? What gives life purpose? These questions are what philosophers call teleology, a subject which is typically dismissed by science as the realm of religion or personal belief systems. This dismissal is fair precisely because of the historical, sociocultural conditions in which the scientific revolution emerged during the late 17th and early 18th centuries of the European Enlightenment. The new scientific way of thinking was initially a reaction against religion's monopoly on meaning, especially regarding understanding and engineering the systems of the world.

The split between religion and science was defined by science becoming newly responsible for the workings of material world and religion's scope being redefined as being responsible for everything immaterial or immeasurable, including matters of teleology.

This tacit separation allowed science to expand and its corresponding engineering knowhow in turn to fuel the industrial revolution. The human population on Earth exploded 1200% since the split occurred between science and religion.

This development has been great for the proliferation of our species, and the conversion of the biosphere into either humans or human food. However now in the 21st century, we are colliding with the limitations of the planet and the assumptions of the standard worldview. Many are starting to realize that the worldview is both incomplete and inconsistent.

What if there is more to reality than we can weigh and measure in the world? Religion, as the historical repository of the world's traditions and organized systems of belief, is not rationally equipped to freshly interrogate immaterial realms—and neither are disorganized pre-rational systems of belief, which have sprung up and proliferated recently.

As helpful as it has been, we threw the baby out with the bathwater. Now we need to take the original thesis of religion and its antithesis of science and synthesize them into a new way of thinking, which transcends both and yet still includes these earlier ways of knowing. This book is a proposal for just such a new way of thinking.

We ignore the core human drive for meaning at our peril. Consider, for example, the rise in nihilism, which is the logical outcome of literally believing that meaning is irrelevant. The stance of nihilism is essentially that human morals and values are forms of vanity, knowledge and communication are impossible, and that life itself is meaningless. Nihilism does not end well.

Several countries are being led by or were recently led by individuals who many psychiatrists have publicly diagnosed with malignant narcissism or narcissistic personality disorder,[6] It should go without saying that it is particularly dangerous for nations to be led by individuals who have psychiatric disorders, but here we are. The fact that societies elect such leaders reflects that their populations do not perceive the real dangers of individuals who find meaning only in themselves. This situation points to a systemic crisis with the standard worldview in assuming meaning is irrelevant.

The recent rise in the uptake of superhero entertainment highlights the core drive to ascribe concrete meaning to the abstract complexity of the world. This drive will assert itself from the depths of the human psyche through organized or disorganized systems of belief whenever necessary to maintain sanity and make life worth living.

Constructing an epistemology which rationally includes teleology supports seekers of meaning and opens a new space for belief and reason to support rather than deny each other. My hope is that this may eventually be incentive enough to start building a sustainable, sane civilization.

---

[6] https://bit.ly/3vylQi2

Ignorance is Strength

Many do not think much beyond concrete appearances. Why bother learning anything if the world's information is always at your fingertips through your smartphone?

Those who do delve deep into the noosphere may be frustrated by the fact that the standard worldview, and the assumptions underlying it, do not really hold together as a coherent philosophy. Are we just consumers?

Yes, we love our smartphones, but the human population has more than doubled in this author's lifetime, and we now face so many systemic problems. Many of us have mentally checked out, retreated into escapism, substance abuse, or suffer from debilitating depression at a time when we really need everyone to be at their best to creatively solve these global problems which affect us all. It is like we are living more and more in an Orwellian nightmare and many have already given in to believing the mind-control slogans of big brother.

Distrust of education and educated people is rising in popularity. Ignorance is not strength but weakness that can be remedied through education.

Education is learning what you didn't even know you didn't know.

Daniel Boorstin (1914-2004) was an American historian and proponent of consensus history.

Anti-intellectualism goes beyond the increasing challenge of affording higher education. Without any education people are basically tribal, unable to understand or sustain complex civilization at anywhere near the current level.

If you think education is expensive, try ignorance.

Derek Bok (1930-) was a former president of Harvard University.

Education does not necessarily have to take the shape of a massive outpouring of time and money to earn a degree from an elite university that may or may not yield a reasonable return on investment. If the traditional academic route is out of reach, pursuing other means to educate yourself is well worth the effort. There are so many free or reasonably priced alternatives today such that education need not depend on money. In this light, education is a personal commitment to discover new ways of thinking and experience whole vistas of knowledge that you were not aware of before.

The mind is not a vessel to be filled but a fire to be ignited.

Plutarch (46-119 AD) was a Greek Middle Platonist, historian, and priest at the Temple of Apollo at Delphi.

If you have read this far, I am certain that you do not assume ignorance is strength and that you have seen through many of the standard worldview's false assumptions. Obviously, what I am writing about—the sacredness of geometry—is at odds with this worldview, so please read on in Part II to encounter a new way of thinking and a much more hopeful outlook.

Part II: A New Way of Thinking

This unified alternative worldview is experienced as three simultaneous philosophical streams in the ontology (chapter 4), epistemology (chapter 5), and teleology (chapter 6). Taken together, this trinity comprises a new way of thinking.

4 | Ontology – Study of Being

Ontology is the experience of being. Although being is absolute, mind is relative. This chapter clarifies what they are and describes the essential relationship between them.

The Absolute

The absolute has no divisions, qualities, or limitations. The absolute is non-temporal, non-local, and infinite. The sole philosophical "ultimate" which exists is awareness, except that awareness is not an object we can weigh or measure but is the actual experiencing you are doing right now.

If the doors of perception were cleansed, everything would appear as it is, Infinite. For man has closed himself up, till he sees all things through narrow chinks of his cavern."

William Blake (1757-1827) was a Romantic poet and visionary artist.

The vacuum of spacetime is probably the closest metaphor for awareness, but even complete nothingness represents a place and time in a finite universe, subject to various field effects such as gravity, electromagnetism, and the laws of physics. Awareness is radically empty beyond even the metaphor of utter nothingness—awareness is the infinity before—beyond—within space and time.

Awareness and Consciousness

In this ontology, awareness and consciousness are interchangeable, synonymous terms. I do not make relative distinctions between these terms in describing the absolute.

Language can only point to awareness because awareness cannot ever be fully defined in language. Awareness is the comprehension of meaning outside language. All such attempts at definition are ultimately relative to mind's necessity to cast unfiltered experiencing into subjects, objects, and predicates. Awareness is the unmistakable experience beyond words—beyond all attempts to characterize the un-characterizable. Mind sees awareness as a paradox, but that is who you are.

Misnomers of Consciousness

We commonly use the word *unconscious* to refer to states of awareness other than being awake and alert. A person can be said to be unconscious when lost in their imagination (daydreaming) while awake, dreaming while sleeping, in deep sleep, intoxicated, or in some other altered state.

The word "unconscious" assumes that it possible to experience the complete lack of consciousness or that you can have greater or lesser amounts (levels) of consciousness. Consciousness has no levels, gradations, compartments or any such divisions. The different states we experience such as waking, dreaming, and deep sleep are all experienced consciously. When you are having a dream, you are consciously experiencing the dream, your dream body and dream world. In deep dreamless sleep, awareness is still present being aware of breathing and other mental activity that is much harder but still possible to access in memory later. In near-death experiences, where no brain activity was measured (the state of brain death), awareness can still have rich phenomenal experiences.

The reason we commonly put gradations on consciousness is a function of the waking state's difficulty of translating memories experienced in other worlds. Have you ever woken up in the morning, not aware of having had a dream until later that day when something triggered the memory? Then you remembered being aware of your dream body and/or dream world, replaying a shadow of the experience again in your mind and waking state brain.

The challenge you have in recalling the dream in your visible world brain is because your soul experienced the dream in the invisible world of the collective human soul, what Psychiatrist Carl Jung called the "collective unconscious," a transpersonal realm of archetypes common to all humanity.

The term Jung chose is problematic for this ontology because it connotes an ambiguous collective lack of consciousness. I prefer the phrase "collective human soul," which is closer to Plato's term which Jung himself preferred, the *anima mundi* or world soul.

We commonly use the terms *subconscious* or *unconscious* synonymously to refer to cognitive processes which take place outside the loop of self-reflective consciousness.

When you drive an automobile, you often do so sub- or unconsciously. Consider when you are thinking about other things, listening to music, daydreaming, or talking on the speakerphone while driving. Lots of cognition goes on making all the many split-second calculations and eye-ear-brain-hand-foot coordination necessary to drive a car. You are always conscious of all these processes, but experienced drivers might not be self-reflectively aware of them. A better term might be "right-brained cognition" or "subliminal cognition."

For all the above reasons I try to avoid using the terms *unconscious, collective unconscious, subconscious,* and *developing your consciousness* (common in self-help books) in favor of other ways of describing the same phenomena, for maximum clarity in thought and expression.

Discovering Your True Identity

By honestly answering a few self-reflective questions, you should be able to easily find out who you really are in just a few minutes. Before you start, I want to define a few simple terms to avoid potential confusion:

- *Sensations* are what you experience through sights, sounds, smells, tastes, touches which include any feelings you have on your skin and inside your body (known as interoception) including sensations felt in your heart.

- *Perceptions* of the world arise as interpretations of sensations. For example, you might perceive a purring cat sitting on a table as the interpretation of various sensations coming from your eyes and ears. Perception is a secondary level of information processing. Emotion is the form of perception commonly known as feeling.

- *Conceptions* arise from sensation, perception, other conceptions, or some combination of these streams. Conceptions can be a tertiary level of processing on sensation, but we often have complex conceptions about other perceptions and conceptions recalled from memory and mixed. For example, you may think, "The cat shouldn't be on the kitchen table! She never listens when I tell her to get down" (remembering and feeling frustration). I will have to move her before dinner, but isn't she cute? (thinking about the future but also feeling love in the moment). Conception is commonly known as thinking but can also mix in feeling—so head and heart.

This is not meant to be a test—just a few easy questions for you to honestly reflect upon and contemplate who you really are. Go ahead and begin the brief self-questionnaire:

1. Do you experience sensations, perceptions, or conceptions coming and going over time?
2. If your sensations, perceptions and/or conceptions come and go over time, do they define who you are right now?
3. If you were asked, "Who are you?" ten years ago, would your answer today be any different?
4. Who are you when you are not telling stories which identify who you were or are?
5. Are you aware—that you are aware—of all thoughts, perceptions, and sensations which you experience?
6. As self-aware awareness, if sensations, perceptions, and conceptions occur in different compartments, channels, or streams within your mind, are these unified in experiencing?
7. Does your contentless awareness have shape, edges, limitations, qualities, or boundaries?
8. Who are you now? Who have you been before and who will you always be?

If your answers were anything like mine, you are the experiencing of being aware of body, mind, and world. You are therefore neither your body nor your mind. This realization is sometimes called "self-realization" because you have become aware of your absolute identity. You are not the person you probably took yourself to be.

It is common to use a kind of shorthand when we talk about you to say that your absolute identity is "awareness" or "consciousness," but these nouns incorrectly objectify you. This is an unavoidable artifact of language. You are subject and object—you are non-local-experiencing throughout time.

How Many Absolutes Exist?

No divisions, qualities or limitations absolutely exist. If there were two (or more) awarenesses that existed separately, then they would each have to be bounded by some quality or limitation, which violates the very definition of what the absolute is.

Even if we ignore the impossible separations, if one awareness became aware of another awareness then they would be in each other's awareness and the separations would have no meaning. The fictitious separations would merge into one awareness having no divisions, qualities, features, preferences, or limitations—again becoming the absolute. The absolute can only ever be universal and unitive.

There is a great taboo in scientific circles and in our culture as a whole against the possibility that consciousness may be universal. Even religion, whose true origin and goal is the understanding of the universal nature of consciousness is deeply prejudiced against this possibility.

Rupert Spira (1960-) is a teacher of non-dual consciousness.

The Relative

The relative is the domain of minds. Minds are modulations of awareness, inseparable from the absolute. The best way to understand the relationship of absolute awareness and relative minds is by analogy.

Awareness is to mind as a screen is to the image projected on it...In other words, in reality, there are not two things—one, the screen and two, the image. There is just the screen. Two things (or a multiplicity and diversity of things) only come into apparent existence when their true reality—the screen—is overlooked. Experience is like that.

Rupert Spira (1960-) is a teacher of non-dual consciousness.

In Rupert Spira's analogy, minds are like finite moving images modulating the screen of infinite awareness. There are innumerable relative boundaries seemingly separating you and the world, between objects in the world, between you and others. These boundaries—also known as names, forms, interiors, or dissociations—are all seamless modulations of the absolute.

The divisions between minds are always relative, like separate images simultaneously projected on the same screen side by side. Being is 100% screen including all its modulation (there is no audience in the analogy), but at the same time, the dramas playing out as separate images on the screen are distinct and interesting to minds in how they relate to one another. Awareness has the absolute infinite capacity to assume the shape and contents of all relative finite minds which modulate its being.

If your relative mind is having problems understanding the absolute you are certainly not alone. If that is how you are feeling, then you are on the right track! Minds cannot ever fully comprehend awareness. Characters in a movie naturally overlook the screen of which they are modulations, but there can be no movie (relative) without the screen (absolute). It takes awareness to know thyself.

5 | Epistemology – Study of Knowing

Epistemology is the study of the origins, nature, and limits of knowledge. In the context of the ontology described in the previous chapter, this epistemology describes the relative domain of minds, which are modulations of absolute awareness.

Minds have divisions, qualities, and limitations which determine mind's unique experience of self. Each mind's qualities—and the relationships minds have with each other—is responsible for the incredible, varied richness of experience.

Each mind is a modulation of awareness, relatively forming content within itself (which is called in-formation, ideas, or knowledge). Each mind has the capacity to communicate information with other minds and interpret knowledge impinging on it from other minds. This flow of ideas creates and sustains complex relationships between minds.

There is only one overarching mind, which I refer to as universal mind. The limited nature of mind necessarily defines a finite boundary which infinite awareness experiences as the sense of *self*. Self-awareness is created by the very act of defining a mental boundary because of the limitations its boundary implies. Awareness experiences a mind's relative limits and mind conceives, "This must be who I am." To mind, information inside its boundary is "me," and information outside its boundary is "not me."

The phenomenon of dissociation is the mechanism by which universal mind subdivides itself into a profusion of minds within. Bernardo Kastrup was the first to figure this out.[1] Dissociation is how awareness experiences different selves with different points of view—always through dissociated minds relating to one another.

Dissociation is a well understood human psychological phenomenon. Dissociative Identity Disorder (DID)[2] is the condition wherein a person hosts multiple dissociated identities (known as alters) within their mind, giving rise to multiple co-conscious inner lives within the same human body. DID is a human scale microcosm of what happens in the macrocosm of universal mind.

Space, time, matter, energy, number, and geometry are all relative conceptions in universal mind. They have no real existence outside awareness.

Number is relative and does not exist separately from a mind.

George Berkeley (1685-1753) created the theory of Immaterialism—a form of idealism—and was also known for his critique of abstraction.

Information impinging on a mind from outside its boundary is what we call *sensation*. Interpretation of sensation within a boundary is *perception*. Additional processing of sensation and perception— and information generated without reference to these inputs, or the admixture of these streams is *conception*. Information within each mind is experienced by awareness in a seamless unity and simultaneously is understood as a trinity.

---

[1] Kastrup, B. (2017). Why Materialism is Baloney.

[2] Dissociative Identity Disorder used to be called Multiple Personality Disorder. Identity is more fundamental that personality.

The domain of universal mind is called the intelligible. Universal mind is dissociated into two subminds: world mind and soul mind. The domains of these top-level subminds are called the visible and the invisible, respectively.

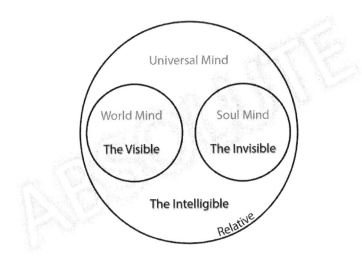

Universal Mind with top-level dissociations, domains, and underlying ontology

The Intelligible Domain

The domain of *universal mind* is called the intelligible. This is the highest mind, transcending all internal dissociations. Conceptions in the intelligible domain are universal and come before-beyond time, space, and the big bang. Intelligible conceptions include mathematics, geometry, logic, the laws of physics, and the "transcendentals," which will be explained shortly.

Behind the world of appearances there is a vast intelligence that creates continuously.

Eckhart Tolle (1948-) is a popular spiritual teacher.

The *intelligible* was given its name by Plato and is essentially what Immanuel Kant called *a priori* knowledge millennia later. Although I have gone with Plato's term here, Kant had basically the same idea in referring to the intelligible domain which comes prior to individual experience and sensation, a domain that we all can access.

It is therefore a question which deserves at least closer investigation and cannot be disposed of at first sight: Whether there is any knowledge independent of all experience and even of all impressions of the senses? Such knowledge is called "a priori" and is distinguished from empirical knowledge, which has its source "a posteriori," that is, in experience.

Immanuel Kant (1724-1804) was an Enlightenment philosopher and is one of the most influential figures in Western philosophy.

Is There One Universal Mind?

There is one universal language, and this is mathematics, which includes number and geometry. This language must have been invented in universal mind to manipulate its intelligible conceptions.

If there were more than one universal mind it follows that there would be more than one universal language. We have not experienced that. There must be only one universal mind.

Mathematics is an independent world created out of pure intelligence.

William Wordsworth (1770-1850) was an English poet.

Universal mind thinks in the language of mathematics that it expressly invented to think, and which sub-minds largely discover. Whether humans invent or discover math is a classic debate. I see this debate as a false dichotomy because both perspectives are correct depending on which point of view one takes.

Modern mathematicians follow the path of the abstract to invent more mathematics which are dissimilar from previous observations of reality, and then at some point in time, those inventions typically end up matching with other forms of reality. This process has been repeated time and time again.

For example, breaking news in 2021 is that the square root of negative one (symbolized by the constant **i**) is essential in describing quantum reality through Schrödinger's wave equation. Previously, physicists went to great lengths to work around using the *imaginary number* **i** — keepin' it real.

The news is this *real number* workaround does not always work, but the imaginary route always does. The imaginary unit—and its ensuing complex numbers—are therefore essential to physical reality[3] (detailed in The Visible Domain).

Although we may assume that humans solely invent math, it is not clear that we are not simply discovering some aspect of what was already there. Let us be honest, humans inventing math is probably hubris, considering that our minds are tiny subsets of universal mind (detailed in The Invisible Domain).

However, inventing math using the human mind is theoretically possible because we have access to the intelligible, universal language. The same creative impulse which motivates our minds also drives universal mind. We are relative co-creators.

---

[3] https://bit.ly/3sa0G7T

Is the Intelligible the Mind of God?

The intelligible is not God unless your mind is also God, because all minds are modulations of awareness. If you and presumably *everyone else* is also God, then the word loses its utility in describing someone specific.

As a dissociative subset, your mind has limited access to the conceptions of universal mind. For example, you doubtless know what a triangle is and understand the equation 1+1=2. However, we do not understand all possible math (which seems infinite) or see how math all fits together, just some of its many pieces. We intuit a far greater scope to universal mind than we can probably even imagine within human minds.

It makes some sense to characterize our access to the intelligible as "God within you" or "you within God," but this not particularly helpful to understanding. After all, you transcend and include the relative mind of God because you are absolute awareness. God is an abstraction in you. Please do not burn me at the stake for pointing this out!

Who is Universal Mind?

When we meditate, we tend to have no words—just the blissful experience of being aware. If universal mind were to meditate and reflect on its identity and then later articulate that inner experience, I speculate that it might identify as truth, beauty, and/or bliss— because these map to our conceptions, perceptions, and sensations of the intelligible. This "unified trinity" is also known as the "transcendentals."

The transcendentals are universally intelligible and paradoxically form both a unity and a trinity. Wherever you experience one transcendental you simultaneously experience the other two.

Check each of the following in your own experience:

- Where there is truth, there is also beauty and bliss.
- Where there is beauty, there is also bliss and truth.
- Where there is bliss, there is also truth and beauty.

The beauty of one form is akin to the beauty of another, and that beauty in every form is one and the same.

Plato (428-348 BC) was a philosopher and pivotal figure in the history of Western philosophy.

We all know transcendent beauty when we see it—beyond cultural conditioning and relative conceptions of beauty. There is transcendent beauty in a triangle. Bliss is the sensation of transcendent, absolute being. What Plato described as goodness we might also call happiness, which is an echo of transcendent bliss.

If you want to be happy, be.

Leo Tolstoy (1828-1910) is widely regarded as one of the greatest authors of all time. His ideas of non-violent resistance had a profound impact on Gandhi and Martin Luther King, Jr.

Transcendent truth likewise exists. For example, the golden ratio is presumably the same everywhere in the universe.

Even if you are only a minority of one, the truth is still the truth.

Mohandas Gandhi (1869-1948) led the campaign for India's independence from British rule through non-violent resistance.

Sometimes people who are searching for one transcendental, recognize it through another. For example, Frank Wilczek, who received the Nobel Prize in physics in 2004 for his work on the strong force, was ostensibly searching for truth in the microcosm of the world but ended up finding it only by recognizing its beauty.

Something I love about Frank's work is that he uses beauty as a criterion for scientific theories. He looks for theories that have beautiful equations, symmetrical, elegant equations that follow certain constraints and broad principles. And what's so really astonishing about this criterion is that, sometimes…it actually works.

Steven Strogatz, podcast host at quantamagazine.org

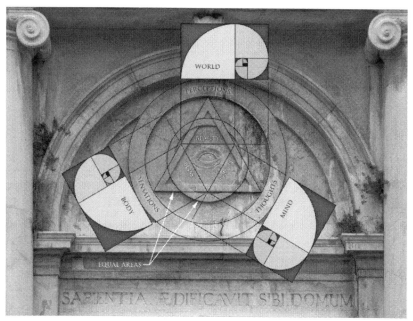

Photo of Santa Maria della Maddalena in Venice by the author. The Latin inscription reads, "Wisdom has built her house." Diagram of unified trinity mirrors structure of minds.

We all know the transcendentals when we experience them because they are the intelligible universal mind self-reflecting on its identity as awareness. One could say the transcendentals are God's highest conceptions pointing to being.

All minds follow the blueprint of being unified as a whole, but on introspection also experience three mental information streams, namely conceptions, perceptions, and sensations.

Pythagoras taught that 3 is the first true number. Plato's student Aristotle claimed that 3 is the first number to which the term "all" applies. These statements make sense in describing a unified trinity.

Geometry is a uniquely direct way to access the universal mind of the intelligible. We can all access this highest relative mind in absolute awareness. Experiencing geometry qualitatively is a self-reflection on the essence of the universal language.

The activity of self-reflection in universal mind eternally and non-locally points to awareness. Therefore, we experience *the sacredness of geometry* because it is imbued with the qualities of the transcendentals.

The Visible Domain

The domain of *world mind*[4] is the visible. The universe (including matter-energy, spacetime, and everything resulting from the big bang) is visible as the exterior products of world mind's inner unified trinity. This interior trinity can be inferred from the fundamental exterior unified trinities of time (past, present, future), space (length, width, depth), and matter (proton, neutron, electron).

---

[4] World mind encompasses not only the world of Earth, but the entire universe.

We sense, perceive, and think about world mind as the physical world we live in. Physics pertains to the visible and yields empirical scientific information, which is what Kant called *a posteriori* knowledge—coming after individual experience. The visible can be weighed and measured, tested, verified, and engineered.

In a reasonable theory there are no numbers whose values are only empirically determinable.

Albert Einstein (1879-1955) is widely acknowledged to be one of the greatest physicists of all time.

This epistemology does not invalidate anything studied by science. Studying the visible domain is essential—but so too is studying intelligible and invisible domains of mind.

Reductive physicalism (also known as materialism) claims that only what is visible exists. Chapter 3 reviewed some of the problems that this gross simplification entails, not least of which is that the visible is built out of the intelligible language of consciousness.

Philosophy is written in this grand book, the universe, which stands continually open to our gaze. But the book cannot be understood unless one first learns to comprehend the language and read the characters in which it is written.
It is written in the language of mathematics, and its characters are triangles, circles, and other geometric figures without which it is humanly impossible to understand a single word of it.

Galileo Galilei (1564-1642) was an astronomer, physicist and engineer best known as "the father of the scientific method."

When we use geometry quantitatively, we are using the language of the intelligible to measure and adjust our invisible perceptions against the relative truth of the visible world. When they match up, we get anything from physics theories to architectural plans attempting to mathematically model, predict and engineer the nature of world mind.

Our experience hitherto justifies us in believing that nature is the realization of the simplest conceivable mathematical ideas.

Albert Einstein (1879-1955) is widely acknowledged to be one of the greatest physicists of all time.

The Microcosm

Quantum physicists discovered a century ago that every quantum entity exhibits a wave-particle duality that is inseparable from consciousness.

For those who are not shocked when they first come across quantum theory cannot possibly have understood it.

Niels Bohr (1885-1962) made foundational contributions to quantum theory and received the Nobel Prize in physics for them in 1922.

Heisenberg's uncertainty principle states that something (in particular, paired matter/anti-matter particles, also known as *virtual particles*) arise from nothing only if they annihilate each other and return to nothing in too short an interval in which to be observed. Consequently, virtual particles dance about the boundary between something & nothing—evidence of visible-invisible domain interaction in my view.

Far from being rare or exotic events, virtual particles permeate spacetime, meaning they are literally everywhere. Amazingly, all the forces of the universe are carried by these virtual particles. The very illusion of substance in the world is continually mediated by massless, chargeless, dimensionless, unobservable, invisible virtual particles.

Electromagnetism and gravitation diminish over distance precisely because higher energy virtual particles are only allowed by the uncertainty principle to exist for comparatively shorter periods of time and therefore cannot travel in space as far as lower energy ones. For example, the forces of gravity and electromagnetism are inversely proportional to the square of distance from their sources, a simple mathematical relationship.

The miracle of the appropriateness of the language of mathematics for the formulation of the laws of physics is a wonderful gift which we neither understand nor deserve.

Eugene Wigner (1902-1995) was a theoretical physicist who received the Nobel Prize in physics in 1963 for his contributions to the theory of elementary particles.

The Macrocosm

All the big stuff of the macrocosm is built out of the small stuff of the microcosm. As the Big Bang theory goes, the entire visible universe suddenly sprang into existence from a *singularity*—a dimensionless mathematical point before space, time, and the laws of physics existed.

Modern science is based on the principle, "Give us one free miracle and we'll explain the rest."

Terence McKenna (1946-2000) was a writer and psychedelic explorer.

The creation story which says everything came from nothing can only have come from the intelligible domain of idea. The visible world—and everything in it—is still an idea, 13.8 billion years later. **Matter** is made of nothing but the mathematical **pattern** of universal mind, the mother and father of the visible.

- **mater** (Latin): *mother*
- **pater** (Latin): *father*

Our external physical reality is a mathematical structure.

Max Tegmark (1967-) is a contemporary physicist known for his mathematical universe hypothesis.

Precisely because the entire visible universe emerged from a singularity, everything is necessarily entangled at the quantum level. Quantum entangled particles form an interconnected whole no matter how far apart they are in space or time.

The essential feature of quantum interconnectedness is that the whole universe is enfolded in everything, and that each thing is enfolded in the whole.

David Bohm (1917-1992) was one of the most significant theoretical physicists of the 20th century.

World Mind Probably Has an Inner Life

Comparing a human neural network with a simulation of the large-scale structure of the universe, we see striking parallels. Both pictures below show the visible exteriors of information processing networks. The characteristic filamentous branching structure is the most efficient way in which organic networks grow their connections.

Both information processing networks appear at vastly different scales and operate on vastly different timeframes. The clear self-similarity of form highlights the fractal quality of recursively dissociated minds. The human brain is a tiny subset of the universe, but it shares a similarly efficient information processing structure. These exterior forms correlate with their invisible interiors. Just as you have an inner life, symmetry suggests that so too does world mind.

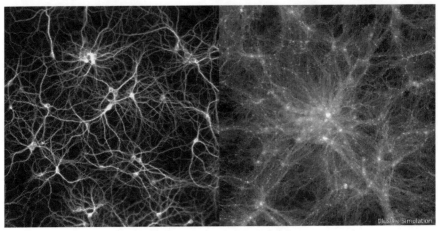

Human neural network (left); simulation of the large-scale structure of the universe (right)

By looking at exteriors alone we might conclude that consciousness is an illusion. However, as stated in Chapter 3, illusionism fails to account for our own first-person conscious experience.

You know that your brain is the visible exterior (a hunk of meat or third-person object) of your corresponding invisible interior mind that you undeniably experience (as first-person subject). Imagine that this does not only just happen with human brains and minds but with additional information processing networks such as the universe and its corresponding interior.

If we examined your brain's neural network under a microscope there would be no more evidence of consciousness in its nodes and pathways than the roadways connecting cities, towns, and villages of France in satellite imagery, or the filamentous superclusters, galaxies, and stars of the universe seen through the telescope—all of which appear to simply be pathways connecting nodes in an organic, efficient manner.

What gives rise to any first-person experience of an interior is simply not present in the visible domain. Your mind cannot be weighed or measured because it is in a sister invisible dissociation within universal mind, which the visible dissociation does not have direct access to (whose relationship is detailed in The Invisible Domain).

World Mind is Recursively Dissociated

We do not tend to have direct access to minds other than our own. I am not aware of your thoughts, for example. The philosophy here is not solipsism because I am not claiming that everything exists inside my individual mind. We non-solipsists recognize other humans and animals are truly conscious and have minds of their own. I speculate that the universe is minded but I do not know that in the same way that I know my own mind. The universe's mind is outside my, and presumably your, individual mentation. However, just as you appear to be conscious, so too do my cats, the planet, and the universe for that matter.

As mentioned earlier, the mechanism by which universal mind takes different points of view must be through dissociation. If universal mind can dissociate once and form world mind, it can do so again through recursion. Recursion is defined in terms of itself as:

Recursion: see *Recursion.*

The above fictional dictionary definition is literally true, but it is something of a joke because it does not really explain the phenomenon.

Another way of understanding recursion is through the following quote:

As above, so below, as within, so without, as the universe, so the soul.

Hermes Trismegistus (2nd century BC), purported author of the Hermetica, ancient writings which influenced the Renaissance.

Typically shortened to simply "as above, so below," just that much of the quote is enough to contain the essence of recursion. Any closed boundary formed within a mind unavoidably creates a submind, which in the act of bounding creates the new self. As awareness takes the new shape, the new submind says, "I am" and defines itself in terms of its perceived limitations.

Did you know that an infinite number of numbers exist between 0 and 1? Consider the concept of the reciprocal, or unity divided by a variable number (1/x). As the number x gets larger, the smaller each subdivision gets as the recursions approach 1. Infinities exist between every number in the intelligible.

Therefore, there is an infinite amount of intelligible space to form nested minds within. If you can imagine this, then it is no stretch to imagine a profusion of dissociated minds within any one mind.

All dissociations are relative and have no real existence outside awareness. However, I am aware of at least the following relative hierarchy of dissociations within world mind:

universe / galaxy / star / planet / body / cell / atom / quark

This linear hierarchy is only part of the picture. Single celled amoebas, atoms, and quarks clearly exist outside bodies. Essentially the listed hierarchy is only one branch of the world mind, which probably is yet another example of the filamentous branching structures mentioned earlier.

I do not know how many of these levels of subminds may be fictitious, or if I am missing some levels, for example superclusters of galaxies. Free floating quarks of any flavor do not exist anywhere and yet within every neutron and proton, three valence quarks and a profusion of four other types of virtual quark/anti-quark particles pop in and out of the visible. A simplified perspective which ignores sub-atomic reality takes world mind at 100% atoms, but this is really a holdover from Democritus (460-370 BC) and his atomic theory of the universe.

A physicist is just an atom's way of looking at itself.

Niels Bohr (1885-1962)

I think Bohr must have been half-joking, but such gross atomic simplification ignores the richness and diversity of experience and is utterly impractical. Consider one or more dissociations can happen at each level in the hierarchy of world mind. For example, there are more than 7 billion human bodies in world mind on planet Earth right now, for example. We certainly take each human body as a separate boundary.

Were you aware that 100% of the atoms comprising each body are swapped out and exchanged with other atoms, all within a year's time? If you take atoms as "ultimates" of being, then recognizing people as valid containers of meaning does not make any sense because we are ephemeral patterns of atoms at best.

The reason we recognize bodies as valid boundaries has nothing to do with the discrete collections of mostly carbon, oxygen, nitrogen, and hydrogen comprising them, but everything to do with the individual invisible souls which animate their corresponding visible bodies. If you have ever seen a deceased person or pet, it is striking how utterly devoid of soul (aka presence) bodies are in death.

The Invisible Domain

Recall that the intelligible universal mind is compartmentalized into two primary dissociated minds, the visible world mind, and the invisible soul mind.

Soul mind interacts with world mind in a sort of partnership or dance, animating universal mind. We cannot weigh or measure the soul in the visible but can feel its invisible presence. Soul is what breathes life into the world on all levels.

Soul Mind is Likewise Recursively Dissociated

Like world mind, soul mind is also recursively dissociated, but not necessarily with the same levels. There is typically one-to-one correspondence between your individual body in the overarching world mind and your individual soul in the overarching soul mind.[5]

As a nested self-similar microcosm of higher ordered minds, the structure of the human brain is a useful analogy. The human brain's left and right hemispheres are to universal mind's world and soul dissociations as the corpus callosum is to the intelligible domain.

---

[5] In cases of dissociative identity disorder in a human individual, more than one soul interacts with a single body.

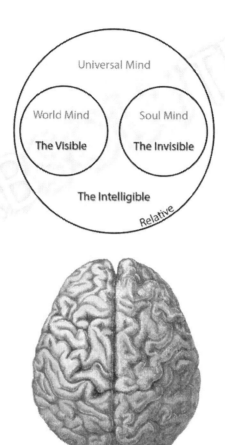

The physiology of the human brain is an analogy to the structure of universal mind.

The human brain is a useful analogy, but is not a literal truth—the brain, its hemispheres and corpus callosum exists entirely in the visible mind while the soul exists entirely within the invisible mind. Universal mind provides the language governing their operation and interconnection.

The Nature of Brain and Mind

The brain's neural network has a filamentous branching structure, optimized to act as an information processing network. It consists of many electrical pathways interrupted by synapses.

One synapse, by itself, is more like a microprocessor with both memory-storage and information-processing elements than a mere on/off switch. In fact, one synapse may contain on the order of 1,000 molecular-scale switches. A single human brain has more switches than all the computers and routers and Internet connections on Earth...There are more than 125 trillion synapses just in the cerebral cortex alone. That's roughly equal to the number of stars in 1,500 Milky Way galaxies... The brain's overall complexity is almost beyond belief.[6]

Stephen Smith, professor of molecular and cellular physiology at Stanford University

That is an amazing amount of complexity in your head, which certainly puts even the most complicated things humans ever create into perspective.

However, let us not get lost in the stars and instead consider that on a qualitative level, no matter how many miles of pathways and whatever number of connections are in the brain, it is electrically short circuited. What determines which switches turn on or off and what gets stored in memory? The modern understanding of the brain is more complicated than the mill Leibnitz described in the 18th century (page 25), but there still is not anything there which would explain a perception.

I think of the brain like a TV that tunes into the station of your invisible mind or as an invisible filter that limits the vast information flow in the overarching soul mind to the trickle of sensations, perceptions, and thoughts specific to your individual soul, informing your first-person experience.

---

[6] https://stan.md/31iDTuR

Quantum processes within neurons must be what constitutes the interface between invisible minds and visible brains. The discovery of quantum vibrations in *microtubules* inside brain neurons has been corroborated by anesthesiologist Stuart Hameroff and Sir Roger Penrose (Nobel laureate in physics, 2020).[7]

I believe the reason for this is how quantum bits are indeterminate until wave function collapse after which they are deterministic. Thinking is like that.

You may realize in the moment that you have potentially many different thoughts on a subject—and can sense their presence—but then through some subtle mechanism, your mind chooses one thought over another. It is what we commonly mean when we say we have made up our minds. After each such mental choice (analogous to a wave function collapse) a train of deterministic thoughts propagate through the brain.

Thoughts are Not Sourced in the Brain

I claim that thoughts and memories do not originate in the brain at all. They are sourced and stored in the invisible domain of your individual mind and consciousness chooses which thoughts to deterministically propagate through your visible brain.

Consider the extreme cases of people with almost no brain matter living normal lives. Finally, here is something that really explains your colleagues!

Joking aside, many documented cases exist of a condition called hydrocephalus in which cerebrospinal fluid becomes trapped in the brain instead of circulating around it.

---

[7] https://bit.ly/3lM9qi0

In one classic example the late Dr. John Lorber, professor of pediatrics at Sheffield University, examined a bright young mathematics student (tested with an IQ of 126). The student was referred to him because the campus doctor noticed that the student's head seemed a little larger than normal.

"Dr. Lorber examined the boy's head by Cat-scan to discover that the student had virtually no brain. This student had a layer of cerebral tissue less than 1mm deep covering the top of his spinal column."[8]

Doctors who are confronted with people leading normal lives without brains are at a complete loss to explain it based on the standard worldview's false assumption that the visible brain must absolutely be where cognition takes place.

We can weigh and measure the brain but not the mind or the soul of which the mind is only a part.

If your soul has an individual mind that interfaces with your brain, it should not be too much to imagine an entire invisible body which likewise interfaces with your physical body.

Asian spiritual traditions going back thousands of years speak of chakras or invisible energy centers corresponding with specific parts of the visible body.

Of course, chakras are dismissed and even ridiculed by science because these cannot be weighed or measured in the visible. Our understanding is all the poorer for this unnecessary reductionism. If brain and mind can exchange information across the dissociative boundaries separating world and soul minds, then it stands to reason that other areas of the body may be able to do so as well.

Our visible and invisible bodies are continually interacting. The soul animates the body which serves as its vehicle in the visible.

---

[8] https://bit.ly/3soxSsy

The Invisible Structure of Mind

Sensations, perceptions, and conceptions were defined in Chapter 4 to assist you in transcending your mind and discovering your absolute identity as awareness. Each one of these mental channels of information is not readily distinguishable by studying electromagnetism in the brain.

In other words, your brainwaves are not like the 3-phase high voltage electricity supplied to industry, with each leg always out of phase with the other two. Instead, this trinity is available only through subjective introspection because it is sourced from the invisible domain of your mind.

Human language echoes the invisible unified trinity of our minds by requiring us to construct complete sentences by including separate subjects, objects, and predicates.

We naturally mirror the structure of our minds in governments, which are designed to act like the minds of the body politic. For example, consider how democratic governments tend to be divided:

- Branches: executive, legislative, judicial
- USA: federal, state, local
- Canada: national, provincial, municipal
- Ancient Rome: consuls, senate, assembly

Religions also often encoded the invisible structure of mind in their traditions and most sacred protagonists:

- Ancient Egyptian: Osiris, Isis, Horus
- Hinduism: Shiva, Brahman, Vishnu
- Christianity: Father, Son, Holy Spirit
- Buddhism: Great retreat which lasts 3 years, 3 months, and 3 days.

Plato's transcendentals of truth, beauty and goodness are an echo of the older Vedic tradition's Sat (truth), Chit (beauty), Ananda (bliss). In discussing the intelligible domain, I used the English translation of the Vedic in characterizing the structure of universal mind's unified trinity as: truth, beauty, and bliss.

Other Invisible Minds

The invisible nature of minds makes them the focus of subjective introspection, which typically cannot be verified with scientific instruments that objectively measure the visible world.

In other words, we cannot use telescopes, microscopes, or Cat-scans to investigate the hierarchy of soul mind's dissociative alters.

You obviously have access to your individual soul mind, which I will often simplify by calling it your *soul* or *psyche* or just (unspecified) *mind*. World mind impinges on us all in the waking state and through it, other people you meet or Zoom with, but you may also receive subtle influences from other invisible souls which may not have obvious visible correlates.

Mental contents inside an alter of universal consciousness cannot directly evoke mental contents outside the alter, or vice-versa. But they can still influence or impinge on each other.

Bernardo Kastrup is a leading contemporary thinker in the philosophy of idealism.

In scientific literature, *anecdotal evidence* (also known as subjective experiences or stories) may be cursorily discussed to give flavor or background, but anecdotes are widely viewed as tantamount to nonsense.

Reflexive dismissal of the subjective will not get us anywhere in understanding the invisible domain. We require a new way of thinking to consider anecdotes seriously as evidence. To study the invisible, here are my recommendations:

- Open your mind, but "not so open that your brain falls out," as the idiom goes.
- Do not reflexively dismiss what you do not understand, otherwise learning is impossible.
- Respectfully take note of invisible subjective phenomena in others' experiences.
- Do not blindly accept others experiences without critical, rational examination and analysis.
- Where appropriate, use tools and objective methods used in studying the visible to investigate the invisible.

Making the Invisible Visible

We all bring at least some aspects of the invisible domain into manifestation in the visible world every day. Making the invisible visible is set of skills one can learn. These include but are not limited to:

Remembering

Imagine smelling or tasting something, which triggers a specific memory from childhood—perhaps your grandmother's cooking. Years have passed and if asked about it beforehand, you probably would not have remembered anything that specific about it. Somehow the sensation accessed memories in your mind which brought the experience vividly back into your brain to be experienced freshly all over again. It was like grandmother and her delicious cooking was right there in front of you again.

Memory is strange like that. It is likely that you know far more than you remember. With the right triggers, it is possible to remember things you have long forgotten in vivid detail. *This suggests that all experiences are persistently stored in the invisible mind of your individual soul.* Bringing memories from your soul, not currently in your brain, to be experienced once again is a skill that can be learned.

"The Method of Loci, [was] an imaginal technique known to the ancient Greeks and Romans...In this technique the subject memorizes the layout of some building, or the arrangement of shops on a street, or any geographical entity which is composed of a number of discrete loci. When desiring to remember a set of items the subject 'walks' through these loci in their imagination and commits an item to each one by forming an image between the item and any feature of that locus. Retrieval of items is achieved by 'walking' through the loci, allowing the latter to activate the desired items. The efficacy of this technique has been well established."[9]

Learning

In the process of assimilating new concepts, invisible content from the souls of one or more teachers passes into their visible brains as quantum vibrations in microtubules which collapse, triggering deterministic electrical signals, which drive muscles in their bodies that in turn convert the information into speech, writing, or images stored in world mind in the form of lectures, books, pictures, online videos, or live Zoom meetings.

At some point you sense the content within these artefacts of world mind, which your brain turns into perceptions that pass into your soul as conceptions which are stored there. The efficiency you have with both the learning and remembering processes is what is commonly called *intelligence*.

---

[9] O'Keefe, John; Nadel, Lynn (1978). The Hippocampus as a Cognitive Map

Experiencing Qualitative Geometry

In this book's sister course, the author and co-host start by gently engaging participants in the learning process, which can be simplified from the student's perspective in the following way.

The student senses content in world mind (in the form of our Zoom meetings), perceives what is happening in their brains and bodies as they draw. The qualities of the geometry they create on paper establishes a connection between the conceptions they are making in their soul and the language of intelligible universal mind.

After some practice, the student learns how to qualitatively use geometry to establish an intelligible-invisible connection directly between universal mind and their soul mind. Geometry then becomes a doorway that opens to this connection, which feels more like remembering than learning.

The awakening of mathematical consciousness is remembering.

Plato (428-348 BC) was a philosopher and pivotal figure in the history of Western philosophy.

The *sacredness of geometry* can be a surprisingly powerful and unexpected subjective experience which can stimulate creativity and extra-sensory perception.

Creativity

The drive to create is a core impulse that when satisfied is its own reward. Ask successful creators how they did what they did, or where they get their ideas or inspirations from, and ego usually steps in to claim credit.

However, if you are being honest, do you know what your next idea will be, and where it will come from? As I am writing this book, I am continually surprised at what comes out of my fingers as they type.

Consider the possibility that inspired works may come from higher minds, of which your soul is a submind. Information can flow from higher selves into your soul and then manifest into the visible world through your human body which then acts as a channel, medium or instrument of higher intelligence.

One higher self that all humans have access to is our species' transpersonal soul mind. Jungian archetypes exist at this level, the 'gods' which interact with each individual psyche.

Our ancestors probably understood this level of soul mind more richly than we do today, as they sat around hearth fires and told stories about the gods. The current equivalent are streaming services such as Netflix and Disney+ which skillfully manipulate archetypes within our souls in every popular show. That is what moves us.

Many popular shows build their own universes. Consider how The Mandalorian, Game of Thrones, Star Trek, the Marvel Universe, The Witcher, and many other massive creative properties inspire their fans to cosplay, write fan fiction and imagine living their lives within the story as much as possible. It is almost as if the writers of these shows have created subminds within the archetypal soul mind which fans strive to commune with—perhaps they do just that.

Many great writers have attested that their fictional characters seem to take on lives of their own. Writers often do not know what their characters are going to do next until they write the next chapter or episode, making the invisible visible.

Consider the possibility that the default mode network of your brain (correlating with your mind's ego)—and all the clamoring voices it usually keeps under wraps—are all fictional characters, each with their own relative ideas of self.

The one thing the separate self cannot stand is being clearly seen. To see the separate self clearly is to see its non-existence.

Rupert Spira (1960-) is a teacher of non-dual consciousness.

Extra-Sensory Perception

ESP is perception coming from beyond the normal 5 senses. This type of perception can be from your own psyche or the result of direct influence from souls without a corresponding visible body. Each one of the mind's trinity of inputs (sensation, perception, and conception) can be overridden by information coming from other minds. For example, clairvoyance and clairaudience override sight and sound sensations and are what we call extra-sensory perceptions, while clairsentience is direct conceptual transfer from one soul to another.

Children often naturally have these abilities, but they are typically told they have overactive imaginations, or are otherwise discouraged in developing ESP skills—typically motivated out of reasonable adult fears about going against the dominant paradigm.

When you daydream or imagine something, have you ever seen or heard sensations that your body's eyes and ears are not picking up—that is to say, in your mind's eye? This common experience is literally ESP, with data from your mind feeding back into your senses and then back into your mind in a loop. Creativity can likewise involve ESP, except it is not always clear where the inspiration for new ideas comes from, your mind or other minds.

Talented mediums are sometimes those children who grew up encouraged to use ESP, who then as adults may not only communicate with the souls of the deceased, but also communicate with members of your soul family, aka spirit guides. Others come to mediumship later in life.

I have received significant, life-changing information about my soul's journey from spirit guides through many exceptional mediums who have cultivated their unique combinations of ESP skills. As I mentioned in the introduction, my documentary series *Secrets in Plain Sight* came about because of a conversation I had with spirit guides through a medium. What mediums do is real and professional mediums are to be treated with respect and valued like doctors or technical specialists in this author's opinion.

Reincarnation seems more plausible after you have conversed with souls of your deceased loved ones who may share with you their genuine surprise in experiencing "life after death."

States of Mind

Commonly known as "states of consciousness," this phrase is a misnomer because consciousness has no divisions, qualities, or limitations as discussed in Chapter 4. Yet we have all experienced the daily states of waking, dreaming and deep sleep, but perhaps not all of us have experienced altered states. What is going on here?

Rather than being states of consciousness, these are states of mind—which emphatically have divisions, qualities, and limitations.

In the waking state your soul interacts strongly with world mind in terms of its content impinging on your mind and informing you with everyday sensations and perceptions.

In the dream state your soul interacts with the collective human soul and interacts with archetypes and strange characters therein. Your body in the dream negotiates changeable, fluid landscapes of soul mind, neither of which conform to the laws of physics we are accustomed to observing in world mind.

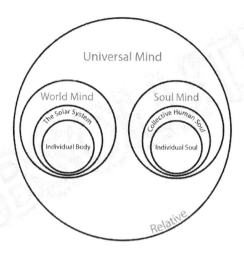

Subminds of the individual and the collective

In deep sleep you pass beyond the boundary of collective human soul and roam within even larger super-minds within soul mind (not depicted) and have experiences you will typically not be able to recall in the waking state. These vast transpersonal experiences can sometimes be recalled through altered states of mentation.

Altered states brought on by near-death experiences, breathwork techniques, or ingesting psychoactive chemicals which interrupt the standard filtering mechanism of the brain have led many to experiencing the rich phenomenology of higher minds.

In 2020, Oregon became the first US state to legalize psilocybin (commonly known as magic mushrooms) for supervised therapeutic use.

A subsequent randomized clinical trial found, "Psilocybin-assisted therapy was efficacious in producing large, rapid, and sustained antidepressant effects in patients with major depressive disorder."[10]

---

[10] https://jamanetwork.com/journals/jamapsychiatry/fullarticle/2772630

I speculate that the reason altered states can bring relief to people suffering from major depressive disorder is how such an experience reveals far more to reality than the standard worldview admits. Its denial of meaning and the consequent rise of nihilism is very depressing and damaging to the human soul. Seeing through such false narratives via altered state mentation is encouraging.

Psilocybes gave our hominid ancestors access to realms of supernatural power, catalyzed the emergence of human self-reflection, and brought us out of the animal mind and into the world of articulated speech and imagination.

Terence McKenna (1946-2000) was a writer and psychedelic explorer.

Although altered states are nothing new, Michael Pollan states in his book How to Change Your Mind, "Today, after several decades of suppression and neglect, psychedelics are having a renaissance." This is true in terms of a new generation studying psychedelics in academia, and the increasing growth of "plant medicine tourism" by many who want to experience these states themselves.

Encountering sacred geometry in altered states is a common experience. Some recognize specific higher-dimensional and non-Euclidean geometries in psychedelic state experiences.[11]

Every time I closed my eyes, snakes, butterflies, owls, panthers and Guacamayo spirits, all made of moving sacred geometry and innumerable colours, soared through my vision.[12]

---

[11] https://bit.ly/3vpi1LS

[12] https://bit.ly/3fMXxGh

Stages of Mind

Commonly known as "stages of consciousness," this phrase is also a misnomer for the same reason "states of consciousness" is incorrect because these are divisions and qualities of relative minds, not indivisible consciousness. Universal mind and all its dissociations are modulations of the absolute. The following diagram is a detail of the individual body and individual soul bubbles shown in the previous diagram, illustrating the visible exterior and invisible interior stages of mind in human development.

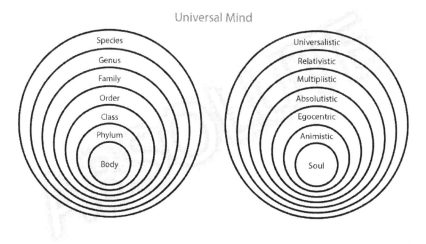

Each individual human mind develops through discrete transpersonal stages.

All the stages shown above exist in transpersonal dissociations. The individual body and soul move through these stages during their development through time. Each successive stage transcends yet still includes its previous manifestations within itself.

The human body develops as a dissociation within world mind in the visible domain. Embryos reflect the course of evolution (not literally recapitulating it), passing through developmental characteristics common to their phylum, class, order early in the developmental process.

These stages are transpersonal minds whose scope includes other species. As we approach the end of gestation, we acquire more qualities of family & genus until finally the qualities specific to our species develop in our mother's womb prior to birth.

The embryo successively adds the organs that characterize the animal classes in the ascending scale. When the human embryo, for instance, is but a simple vesicle, it is an infusorian; when it has gained a liver, it is a mussel; with the appearance of the osseous system, it enters the class of fishes; and so forth, until it becomes a mammal and then a human being.

Karl Ernst von Baer (1792-1876) was the founding father of embryology, whose ideas are the basis of modern evolutionary developmental biology.

The human soul develops as a dissociation within the soul mind in the invisible domain. At birth we are all at an animistic stage, discovering the limitations of our individual soul dissociation which defines what "is me" and eventually that mother and the world are "not me." In early childhood we pass into the egocentric stage which correlates with the development of the default mode network in the visible brain, the "neurological basis for the self." As we develop, the individual progresses through successive levels of collective minds including absolutistic (seeing everything in concrete black and white terms), multiplistic (able to see exteriors in abstract levels which include shades of gray), relativistic (sensitive to interiors and collective ideation), and universalistic (focusing on the good of all).

Although each philosopher's terminology varies, discrete stages of human development were discovered and mapped out by Jean Gebser (1905-1973), Clare Graves (1914-1986), contemporaries Don Edward Beck, Christopher Cowan, Ken Wilber, and many others.

> Different phenomenological worlds, real worlds, come into being with each new level of consciousness development.

Ken Wilber (1949-) is the creator of integral theory, a philosophy which synthesizes the interior and exterior of the individual and the collective.

Our circles of concern increase in scope with each successive stage of soul development from mother (animistic) to self (egocentric), to family, tribe, religion (absolutistic), to guild, corporation, nation (multiplistic), to the environment and intersectionality (relativistic), and eventually to stewarding the health of all living and non-living systems (universalistic). The individual has the capacity to be influenced by each of these collective minds and corresponding worldviews as one's soul develops in time.

Each stage represents a massive fundamental shift in a person's phenomenological world experienced in response to transcending the limitations of the previous stage. However, most human development is arrested at one of the intermediate levels due to challenging life conditions which limit one's circle of concern. Most of humanity is estimated to be in the absolutistic (40% blue) and multiplistic stages (30% orange in Integral recolored terminology). [13]

> No problem can be solved from the same level of consciousness that created it.

Albert Einstein (1879-1955) is widely acknowledged to be one of the greatest physicists of all time.

---

[13] https://bit.ly/3tbxSMT

Much about politics and culture wars stem from complete ignorance of the transpersonal stages of mind. We would all do well to understand and support human developmental processes which are ongoing throughout everyone's lifetimes.

Modes of Mind

Through mental focus alone, we all have access to three separate modes of mentation—contemplation, concentration, and meditation. By using intention and attention to focus in on each aspect of mind's unified trinity, anyone can experience these modes asynchronously:

- Contemplation prioritizes conception (thinking), echoing intelligible truth.
- Concentration prioritizes perception (seeing and coordinating body movements), echoing intelligible beauty.
- Meditation prioritizes sensation (breathing), echoing intelligible bliss.

Our psyche is set up in accord with the structure of the universe, and what happens in the macrocosm likewise happens in the infinitesimal and most subjective reaches of the psyche.

Carl Jung (1875-1961) was an influential psychiatrist.

---

6 | Teleology – Study of Causes

Teleology addresses ends, goals, causes, and purposes—why things seem to happen as they do.

The standard worldview and the alternative worldview have markedly different takes on teleology. My strategy in this chapter is to summarize each worldview's positions on wide-ranging topics, to better compare and contrast their perspectives.

Purpose

Standard Worldview

Only certain animal lifeforms have purpose, the ones which are conscious. Humans have aims, goals, designs, and explanations for many of the things that they do. Animals seem to share in having purposes, but we tend to draw the line at a lower threshold of nervous complexity which can possibly support any form of intelligence. Perhaps a flatworm with a ganglion for a brain or a shrimp might be the lower limit on consciousness, but the line is unclear.

Plants, fungi, protists, bacteria, viruses, and single-celled organisms do not have purposes because they do not have brains, therefore it follows these types of life are unconscious and without purposes.

Alternative Worldview

By virtue of consciousness being the absolute ground of being, all minds which modulate awareness naturally have their own purposes, aims, goals, and reasons appropriate to themselves.

Purpose arises in every sub-mind's relationship to awareness and to other minds in its own quest to try to comprehend its identity and experience.

Far from being a rare, possibly illusory phenomenon, purpose is embedded at every relative level of the intelligible, visible, and invisible domains in every mind and dissociative submind. Minds inherently have purpose.

The World

Standard Worldview

The entire universe is utterly devoid of purpose, except to animals with complex brains. The laws of physics, chemistry, and biology have absolutely no purpose or teleology.

Alternative Worldview

The World has purpose precisely because it is minded. The world is full of recursive sub-minds, brimming with purposes. Although competition has a role, cooperation is the rule amongst world minds. Take biological cells for example. Single celled organisms may compete for limited food sources, while multi-cellular life requires massive cellular cooperation for the larger organism to survive. Minds at cross-purposes (for example those in competition) typically serve higher, evolutionary purposes.

Life

Standard Worldview

In 2011 Edward Trifonov, a Russian geneticist, reviewed 123 definitions of life. After linguistic analysis, all the definitions agreed on one thing, "Life is self-reproduction with variations."[1] Of course, the unexamined assumption is that this definition applies only to biological life observed in the physical world.

---

[1] https://bit.ly/3svZ9t1

Alternative Worldview

Edward Trifonov's discovery of the core definition, "Life is self-reproduction with variations," aptly describes the nature of mind. Minds fit the underlying core definition of life, from universal mind down though all recursive dissociations. Each mind reproduces itself inside new dissociative boundaries which inform each new self, which will necessarily be varied in relationship to all other minds.

The upshot is that the universal, world, and soul minds (and all their recursive dissociations) are alive. Everything is alive and conscious—not just a few animals on planet Earth in some random solar system of a single galaxy.

Evolution

Standard Worldview

The theory of Darwinian evolution posits that the history of biological life in the physical world is the history of genetic mutation arising solely by chance, with mutations conferring advantage conserved by natural selection—no teleology needed.

However, when teaching evolution, it is common to say evolution "made" eyes to sense the world, even though there is no actor named Evolution who made eyes according to its designs, goals, or purposes.

Personifying evolution is done simply for the practical purpose of facilitating human cognition, even though this is technically inaccurate. Some biologists consider teleological language highly problematic, but also unavoidable.

Teleology is like a mistress to a biologist: he cannot live without her but he's unwilling to be seen with her in public.

J. B. S. Haldane (1892-1964) was the "most erudite biologist of his generation."

Alternative Worldview

Structures like eyes evolve for the purpose of seeing. Evolution is irreducibly teleological because it is consciously guided by minds.

The universe was and is continually finely tuned to support maximum complexity and more interesting outcomes by minds at all levels, always using the universal language of the intelligible.

There are mathematical rules that govern the way evolution works.

Arik Kershenbaum, author of The Zoologist's Guide to the Galaxy (2021)

World and soul are co-equal dance partners, simultaneously driving evolution and involution. Evolution is the process by which soul minds drive world minds to adapt to changing conditions, resulting in structural changes in world minds. In the case of biology, invisible souls responsible for entire species drive their corresponding visible body forms to change.

Involution is the opposite process by which world minds drive soul minds to adapt to changing conditions, resulting in adaptation in soul minds. World and soul co-create our experience of this cosmic dance in our corresponding dissociated subminds deep within.

Meaning

Standard Worldview

Religion, ethics, aesthetics, and morality arise from ascribing meaning—but these are all culturally relative pursuits. Some look to organized or disorganized systems of belief to ascribe meaning to their lives, behaviors, and value systems.

"Life has no meaning. Each of us has meaning and we bring it to life. It is a waste to be asking the question when you are the answer."

Joseph Campbell (1904-1987) was an American professor of literature who worked in comparative mythology and comparative religion.

You will have to bring your own meaning to the party because meaning is not found in physics, chemistry, biology, or evolution, present company excepted.

Alternative Worldview

The quest for meaning is a core human drive that motivates us all. Minds naturally seek meaning by trying to comprehend visible and/or invisible minds.

Attempting to understand visible minds is the outer path of science. Attempting to understand invisible minds is the inner path of mysticism.

Spoiler Alert: Both outer and inner paths ultimately lead to the same destination—analogies pointing to consciousness.

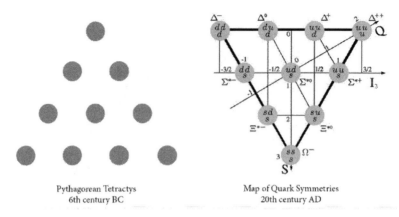

Pythagorean Tetractys
6th century BC

Map of Quark Symmetries
20th century AD

The paths of the mystic (left) and scientist (right) ultimately end up pointing to consciousness.

Meaning cannot ever be completely spelled out in language.

All our reasonings concerning matters of fact are founded on a species of analogy.

David Hume (1711-1776) was a philosopher who sought to understand the psychological basis of human nature.

Meaning can only ever be understood by absolute consciousness, because consciousness is the meaning all its relative modulations are seeking and ultimately made of.

You are not a drop in the ocean.

You are the entire ocean in a drop.

Rumi (1207-1273) is most popular, best-selling poet of all time.

Synchronicity

Standard Worldview

"Synchronicity" is the coincidence of two or more causally unrelated events. Ascribing meaning to synchronicity is spurious. As primates, we have sophisticated visual processing systems in our brains that detect patterns. Our brains can easily be tricked into detecting non-existent patterns such as faces in the bark of a tree or the Virgin Mary in a grilled cheese sandwich. Synchronicity is a belief system conforming to preconceived expectations.

The psychiatrist Carl Jung and physicist Wolfgang Pauli's mid-20th century reflections on synchronicity clearly went beyond the standard worldview[2] and anticipated the articulation of an alternative worldview, of which mine is one possible example.

Alternative Worldview

Causality is one of the most important concepts in physics. The visible world follows rules where causes typically precede effects in time. However, causality can break down under quantum entanglement effects where consciousness is a factor.[3]

Synchronicity messes with our standard notions of causality where meaningful coincidences in seemingly unrelated phenomena noticeably pile up.

---

[2] https://pubmed.ncbi.nlm.nih.gov/15533199/

[3] https://en.wikipedia.org/wiki/Delayed-choice_quantum_eraser#Retrocausality

> All our reasoning is based on the law of cause and effect
> operating as a sequence. The Chinese do not reason so
> much along this horizontal line from past, through present
> to future; they reason perpendicularly, from what is in one
> place now to what is in another place now. In other words,
> they do not ask why, or from what past causes, a certain set
> of things is happening now; they ask, "What is the meaning
> of these things happening at this moment?"

*Lama Anagarika Govinda (1898-1985) was the founder of the Buddhist
order Arya Maitreya Mandala*

Synchronicity can be meaningful if you are open to it. It is
probable that synchronicity is a method invisible minds employ to
signal through the visible world to invisible minds, especially to
individuals who have not developed ESP abilities.

In my personal experience, synchronicity in the world can feel
like it confirms when I am "on the right path" in my inner spiritual
journey.

> Synchronicity postulates a meaning which is a priori in
> relation to human consciousness and apparently exists
> outside man.

*Carl Jung (1875-1961) was an influential psychiatrist and psychanalyst
who founded analytical psychology.*

Synchronicity is an indirect form of communication that is open
to interpretation (and misinterpretation). Seeing synchronicity
everywhere is a symptom of madness, so syncs are best experienced
in moderation.

Consciousness

Standard Worldview

Explaining the existence of consciousness is a "hard problem" because it is ultimately a paradox. Why arrangements of inanimate matter can have animate inner lives remains a mystery.

To say that consciousness emerged at some point in the evolution of life doesn't give us an inkling of how it could emerge from unconscious processes, even in principle.

Sam Harris (1967-) is a reductive materialist and neuroscientist.

Not all materialists see consciousness as paradox, some perceive no problem in its emergence, or simply deny consciousness exists (illusionism).

Alternative Worldview

The one point of agreement between the standard and alternative worldviews is that consciousness seems to be paradoxical. We established in Chapter 4 that consciousness is who you ultimately are. Where do you end—what are the limits which define you?

Is your consciousness limited to the boundaries of your brain or your body? If you see the brightest star in the night sky, Sirius, then does your awareness extend at least that far, some 8.64 light years away? Astronomers have imaged the cosmic microwave background radiation, which depicts the outer boundary of the universe. Knowing this, is your awareness as big as or bigger than the universe?

Consciousness is the ultimate container with infinite capacity. Somehow first-hand we know that nothing can seemingly contain everything. In Big Bang theory, everything somehow sprang out of nothing 13.8 billion years ago. This only makes sense if everything is made from consciousness.

Form is Emptiness. Emptiness is Form.

Buddhist Heart Sutra (661 AD)

Consciousness is no problem at all. You are naturally a paradox. Mind thinks consciousness is a paradox only because the bounded can never fully encompass and understand the unbounded.

I would rather have questions that can't be answered than answers that can't be questioned.

Richard Feynman (1918-1988) received the Nobel Prize in physics in 1965 for the development of quantum electrodynamics.

Multiverse

Standard Worldview

The fact that against all odds, the universe is very finely tuned for conscious biological life exactly as we experience it can be explained by the concept of the *multiverse,* a large or possibly infinite number of alternate physical universes which exist in parallel with our own. The fact that we are conscious in this universe means that we are in one of the few, or possibly the only universe capable of supporting our form of life.

Some physicists raise a red flag with the concept of the multiverse because it cannot be empirically disproved[4], a requirement of the scientific method. Dark matter and dark energy, never having been detected by experiment, also fall into this *unfalsifiable* category.

Alternative Worldview

Nothing violates the principle of parsimony more than the idea of a multiverse. We do not need to believe in an unfalsifiable multiverse any more than we need to believe in an invisible pink unicorn.[5] The hard problem of fine tuning is no problem once we understand that the universe is alive and minded. Minds purposefully fine tune by their very nature.

Universe as Simulation

Standard Worldview

There is a popular idea that we are living in a computer simulation. It probably began with a 2003 philosophical paper by Nick Bostrom.[6]

Astrophysicist Neil deGrasse Tyson and Elon Musk both believe in this simulation hypothesis,[7] which assumes that our descendants will eventually make computers so unimaginably powerful that they will run simulations of their ancestors, which is the universe we are currently experiencing—a simulation like the popular Matrix film franchise.

---

[4] Kragh, H. (2009). "Contemporary History of Cosmology and the Controversy over the Multiverse". Annals of Science. 66

[5] https://en.wikipedia.org/wiki/Invisible_Pink_Unicorn

[6] Bostrom, N. (2003). "Are You Living in a Computer Simulation?". Philosophical Quarterly. 53

[7] https://nbcnews.to/3rz4jmC

The simulation hypothesis would explain things like fine tuning and coincidences such as how the Moon disc perfectly covers the Sun disc during a total solar eclipse as seen from the surface of Earth, precisely during the time intelligent life has emerged to observe it. The Moon is slowly moving away from Earth, so this is temporary.

No other planet/moon combination in our solar system does this. No other satellite is just the right size and distance from its planet to match the size of the Sun as seen from the planet's surface, which is itself determined by that planet's distance from the Sun. The astronomical odds against such coincidences all aligning could be an "Easter egg," or secret undocumented feature in a video game.

If you assume any rate of improvement at all, games will eventually be indistinguishable from reality. We're most likely in a simulation.

Elon Musk (1971-) is one of the richest people in the world.

Alternative Worldview

The idea that we might be living in a simulation is interesting from the standpoint of science fiction and video games. However, if our descendants are running this simulation that we are supposedly living inside of, what is the computer that is running the simulation made of and how are the laws governing it any different than those in the simulation?

Couldn't that "real" world where the powerful computer running the simulation is located also be running inside another simulation within another computer in an even "more real" world?

This argument can go on recursively forever and we never get any closer to discovering what qualities are more real about each successive universe. The argument collapses in a "reductio ad absurdum" type fallacy.

The fact that the Moon disc perfectly covers the Sun disc during a total solar eclipse bears the signature of consciousness—the ultimate experienced reality—more than an "Easter egg," which a video game developer living in a fractionally more real world might encode.

Individual developers might not be able to resist the temptation to sign their creations with their names, likenesses and possibly group affiliations. The Moon-Earth-Sun coincidences involved appear to be anonymous, which lend themselves less to developers in a more real world than a universe in transpersonal consciousness.

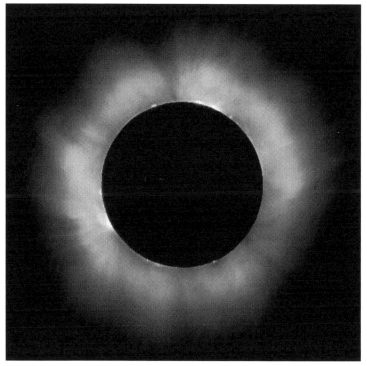

The Moon, Sun, and Earth conspire in the totality of solar eclipse. Image credit: I, Luc Viatour CC BY-SA 3.0

Part III: Sinking In

After reading and assimilating the philosophy in Parts I and II, it may take time to sink in and comprehend its implications, a process that can potentially transform your entire worldview. Part III takes you on a guided tour of some highlights in the visible universe from macrocosm to microcosm in Chapter 7, addresses potential objections your mind may come up with in Chapter 8, and concludes with some choice words and images to contemplate in the final Chapter 9.

7 | As Above, So Below

In this chapter, we are going on a journey through the visible world from its largest to smallest scales to glimpse a few of the many visible secrets in plain sight which imply the interaction of invisible minds.

The Universe

"Fine-tuning" is a hard problem to solve (in addition to consciousness) if we assume that the visible universe is all there is. Physicist Max Tegmark showed that there are 32 dimensionless constants (knobs in the analogy) from which every other fundamental constant of nature can be theoretically derived.[1]

33 controls must have been finely tuned to create our universe including the big bang switch.

---

[1] Tegmark, M. (2015). Our Mathematical Universe: My Quest for the Ultimate Nature of Reality

Some of the knobs must be so incredibly finely tuned to create a universe with stars and atoms, let alone a universe capable of supporting life, that we have truly won the cosmic lottery. In the case of one knob, the dark energy density, the angle must be finely tuned on the order of 123 decimal places or galaxies would not form!

Each one of the many knobs had to be finely tuned prior to the big bang or we would not experience the interesting universe that we do.

If electrons were much lighter, there could be no stable stars, and if they were much heavier, there could be no ordered structures such as crystals and DNA molecules. If protons were 0.2% heavier, they would decay into neutrons unable to hold on to electrons, so there would be no atoms. If they were instead much lighter, then neutrons inside of atoms would decay into protons, so there would be no stable atoms except for hydrogen. Indeed, the proton mass depends on another knob that has a very wide range of variation and needs to be fine-tuned to thirty-three decimal places to get any stable atoms other than hydrogen. Many of these fine-tuning examples were discovered in the seventies and eighties by Paul Davies, Brandon Carter, Bernard Carr, Martin Rees, John Barrow, Frank Tipler, Steven Weinberg, and other physicists. And more examples just kept turning up.[2]

Max Tegmark (1967-) is a contemporary physicist known for his mathematical universe hypothesis.

---

[2] Tegmark, M. (2014). Our Mathematical Universe: My Quest for the Ultimate Nature of Reality

Tegmark and the others listed at the end of the quote are atypical. Many physicists tend to dismiss the problem of fine tuning by deferring to the abstraction of a multiverse comprised of an infinite number of material universes, if they consider it at all. They claim the reason we are even having this conversation is that our singular material universe must have won the cosmic lottery.

By the principle of Occam's razor—which states that the simplest explanation is usually the right one—we can avoid positing an infinite number of physical universes by re-examining the materialist assumptions underlying our conception of the universe in the first place.

In Chapter 5's section, "World Mind Probably has an Inner Life," you saw the image comparing the universe's large-scale structure and the human neural network. If the universe has an invisible soul which interacts with world mind to optimize its partner, then fine tuning is no problem at all—it is simply what minds do to enjoy fuller, more interesting experiences. The universe intentionally fine tunes itself.

What if world and soul minds consciously work together at all levels to not only finely tune the universe, but to finely tune even the microcosm of each galaxy, solar system, living body, every fold of protein, and every base pair of DNA? Infinite consciousness has the capacity to choose and select for more interesting outcomes, supporting ever greater levels of complexity. Awareness simultaneously transcends the world and soul but is also immanent within them, fine-tuning to support fuller matrices of meaning.

Stars

Stars may be the visible physical correlates of invisible souls. Some thinkers have suggested that the magnetic fields of the Sun have a complexity on par with the magnetic fields of a human brain and therefore the Sun may be conscious. I am sympathetic to this view but disagree with the popular advocacy of panpsychism or cosmopsychism to explain why the Sun might be conscious.

Panpsychism is the idea that a primitive form of consciousness resides in small physical things or fields—like Leibnitz's consciousness units he called *monads*, which are separate from atoms. Large combinations of such consciousness units, fields or monads give rise to more complex consciousness. With this logic, an object the size of the Sun would be highly conscious indeed and humans must be less conscious because we are far smaller, and therefore are composed of far fewer of these consciousness units. Some panpsychists ascribe a different level of consciousness to aggregate things like rocks, believing that the experiences of simple, homogenous things must be fundamentally more primitive and discontinuous from the rich experiences of complex heterogeneous things like humans. The question then is where do you draw the line between homogenous and heterogeneous things?

Cosmopsychism takes the opposite approach and posits that only the cosmos is fully conscious, and therefore smaller things within it must be less conscious. Like panpsychists, cosmopsychists[3] also believe that the cosmos exists independently of consciousness.

Both the bottom-up and top-down approaches to locating supposed units and levels of consciousness are fundamentally materialist worldviews, which attempt to explain "the hard problem of consciousness" by passing the buck to either the atomic or cosmic scales, while still inhabiting a physical universe.

---

[3] Nagasawa, Y. and Wager, K. (2016). Panpsychism and Priority Cosmopsychism

In my view, neither philosophy goes far enough. Materialist assumptions run deep, even in many trying to see through them. It is quite a figure-ground shift to realize that the world and everything in it, big and small, are imagined in minds which are nothing but modulations of consciousness. Consciousness is the absolute ground of being—spacetime and magnetic fields are relative ideas. Stars are presumably minded at a specific recursive level within visible and corresponding invisible dissociations of universal mind, just as humans are in microcosm.

Even if stars do not have souls (and my guess is that they do) stars are in-formations of world mind—relative images modulating the screen of consciousness, recalling Spira's analogy from Chapter 4. If stars do have souls, the number of souls in the universe is a truly astronomical number far exceeding the number of stars. What about all the planets revolving around stars and the myriad life forms potentially inhabiting at least some of them?

Planets

Johannes Kepler is best known for his three laws of planetary motion (published in 1619), which we still use today. These laws are:

1. Any planet's orbit is an ellipse with the star at one of its two foci.
2. A line segment joining a planet and the star it orbits sweeps out equal areas during equal intervals of time.
3. The square of a planet's orbital period is proportional to the cube of the length of its elliptical orbit's semi-major axis.

Kepler discovered that three purely mathematical relationships govern the motion of planets around every singular star system in the universe (binary stars also orbit their common barycenter in ellipses). His ideas provided the foundation for Isaac Newton's theory of universal gravitation some 68 years later.

Kepler had an epiphany on July 19, 1595 that regular 2D polygons with inscribed and circumscribed circles representing the orbits of planets might be the geometrical basis of the solar system.

Kepler found that his inspiration did not quite check out, because of the elliptical nature of planetary orbits. He then made a 3D model of nested regular polyhedra inscribed and circumscribed by spheres but was disappointed that it too fell short of perfection.

Geometry is one and eternal shining in the mind of God.

Johannes Kepler (1571-1630) was a mathematician, astronomer, and astrologer.

John Martineau discovered the geometric basis Kepler was looking for by normalizing the planetary elliptical orbits as circular mean orbits.[4] His book is full of fascinating geometries describing planetary orbits, sizes, and movements in time. Here is one example:

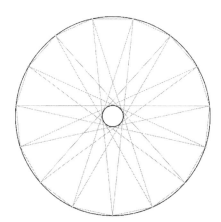

*15-pointed star simultaneously describes the **mean orbits and sizes** of Earth and Saturn (99.8% accuracy). The odds against these unrelated parameters coinciding are astronomical!*

---

[4] Martineau, J. (2002). A Little Book of Coincidence: In the Solar System

Ever since Karl Popper's book <u>The Logic of Scientific Discovery</u> (published in English in 1959), in which he introduced the concept of *falsifiability*, scientists prefer to ignore that Kepler was an astrologer, just as Newton was an alchemist. The subjective domains these heroes of science pursued are not falsifiable because they cannot be contradicted by possible empirical observation.

Therefore astrology, for example, is not considered scientific, in the narrow sense of science being concerned only with empirical data gathered from the visible world.

Astrology is not astronomy, just as alchemy is not chemistry. If science is concerned only with astronomy and chemistry that is appropriate to Popper's narrow scope for science, but we need not discard and denigrate whole subjective domains simply because they do not have an empirical basis.

In terms of history, astronomy grew out of astrology just as chemistry grew out of alchemy. The newer disciplines did not supersede the older, but instead shifted their focus onto different kinds of knowledge, *a posteriori* versus *a priori*, or objective versus subjective.

Astrology is entirely geometric. The natal chart records the positions of the planets at a person's birth in relation to a 12-part equal division of the full circle of stars in Earth's orbital plane into the 12 signs of the zodiac. Aspects between planets are interpreted as being significant when their angles form any conjunction (dot), opposition (line), trine (equilateral triangle), square, quincunx (pentagon), or sextile (hexagon) geometry. Astrology is real.

One is unlikely to discover what one is certain cannot possibly exist.

Richard Tarnas (1950-) is a cultural historian and professor of philosophy and psychology at the California Institute of Integral Studies

---

The Earth and Moon have a remarkably pure geometric relationship. Comparing the actual sizes of these bodies put together, we see that they conform to what is called a Kepler triangle (99.7% accuracy), whose edge lengths conform to the Pythagorean theorem and the golden ratio (symbolized by the Greek letter Φ).

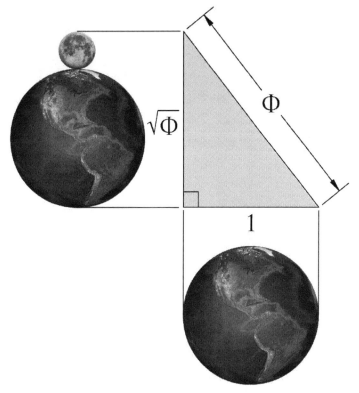

The Earth and Moon's sizes conform to the geometry.

Geometry has two great treasures: one is the theorem of Pythagoras, the other the division of a line into extreme and mean [aka the golden] ratio. The first we may compare to a measure of gold, the second we may call a precious jewel.

Johannes Kepler (1571-1630)

Cities

We do not normally see how a city could possibly have a mind exhibiting some order transcending the individual humans which planned, designed, and built its components. But the spirit of a place, or *genius loci*, may very well have an invisible minded correlate, subtly influencing all the souls of its inhabitants.

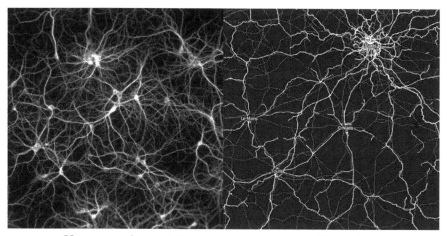

Human neural network (left); organic road networks of France (right)

We all know this qualitatively. For example, Paris feels subjectively different than London, even though they are both large capital cities. If you asked a truck/lorry driver on one of the roads of France if they were part of some larger French super-mind, they would think you were crazy. I suspect that if one were able to ask a single neuron's cellular mind whether it subjectively believed it was part of some larger organism, it would probably also think you were insane, because that is preposterous from its limited point of view.

Taken out of context, the questions do not seem meaningful. However, there could be invisible minded correlates to visible regions and cities which influence their inhabitants. The symmetry of their information processing networks (roads) suggest this might be the case.

Architecture

Marcus Pollio Vitruvius (80-15 BC) wrote the Ten Books of Architecture that proved to be highly influential 1500 years later during the Renaissance. Vitruvius advocated a trio of principles on which to base buildings: strength, utility, and beauty. Interestingly these principles echo the Platonic transcendentals of truth, goodness, and beauty—and how all minds are informed with conceptions, sensations, and perceptions.

Vitruvius detailed the sacred geometric proportions of the human body, "Just so the parts of Temples should correspond with each other, and with the whole." This principle of mirroring the proportions of sacred architecture on the proportions of human body is one used in many religious traditions. The most transcendent architecture proportionally relates the individual to something larger than themselves, making them feel connected and aligned with the cosmos.

Thus, Eliade structures the anthropo-cosmic homology, Body—House—Cosmos…the human becomes microcosm of the house or temple, just as the house or temple becomes microcosm of the cosmos. The inverse is true as well: the cosmos is macrocosm to the house, the house is macrocosm to the human, and the human is, therefore, in profound interrelationship with the cosmos.[5]

Beverly White Spicer, who attended one of my workshops in Ireland.

---

[5] Spicer referred to Mircea Eliade's book The Sacred and the Profane: The Nature of Religion (2001) in this quote from her dissertation: The Ka'bah: Rhythms of Culture, Faith and Physiology

Apparently Roman ideas echoed the earlier Greek conceptions, which in turn recapitulated the ancient Egyptian forms. These ideas may be as old as recorded history.

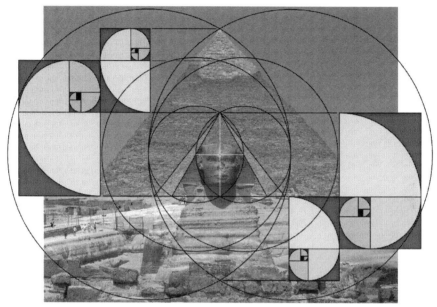

Geometry: the author; Photo: Daniel Mayer CC BY-SA 4.0

Human Body

The most famous depiction of the human body is probably Leonardo da Vinci's Vitruvian Man, where he depicted the proportions Marcus Pollio Vitruvius described in his Ten Books of Architecture.

I discovered that the circle and square in the Vitruvian Man have interesting relationships with the golden ratio, which was first described by Euclid, 2000 years ago. The golden ratio is essentially the mathematical equivalent of the Hermetic statement, "As above so below," in its very definition, which is how the whole segment is to the larger portion in the same proportion as the larger portion is to the smaller portion.

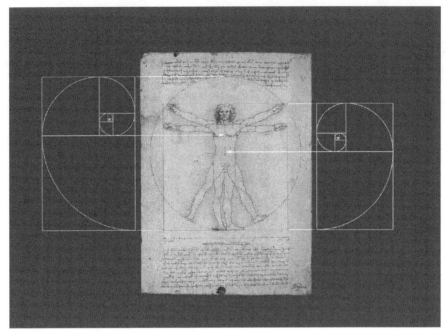

Leonardo's Vitruvian Man overlayed with the author's golden rectangles

The golden ratio is often expressed in two dimensions as a golden rectangle, which has the property of self-similarity baked into its ever-smaller square divisions. These squares can be connected by a series of arcs which approximate a golden spiral that has no mathematical end.

Leonardo da Vinci's Vitruvian Man is circumscribed by both a square and a circle, which in my view represent the body and soul, respectively. The golden rectangle's primary division on the square points to the navel, which marks the center of the body and circle. The golden rectangle's primary division on the circle points to the heart, which is the spiritual center.

My book Secrets in Plain Sight: Leonardo da Vinci (2015) shows how he structured many of his paintings based on golden ratio geometry. I concluded that Leonardo pointed with the golden ratio's divisions to physical and illuminated third eyes, suggesting he saw the divine not just in a transcendent heaven, but immanently in the human body and in the world—a heretical idea in his time.

Humans occupy a scale in visible domain which is at the golden ratio with respect to the macrocosm and microcosm. The size of the visible universe is on the order of 10^{26} meters in size. The size of the proton measures approximately 10^{-16} meters, 42 orders of magnitude smaller. Human scale is approximately 10^{0} or 1 meter. On a logarithmic scale, the whole is to the larger (42/26) as the larger is to the smaller (26/16)—both approximations of the golden ratio.

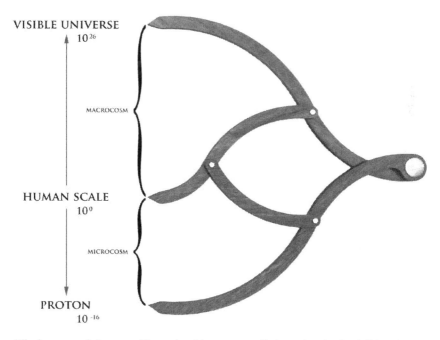

The human scale is at a golden ratio with respect to all that exists in the visible universe.

Incidentally, the handheld instrument depicted is my design called the Proportioner (version 1.0 shown above), which has a middle arm that always proportionately indicates the golden ratio as its arms open and close. I personally manually assemble and send out every Proportioner—a labor of love. The second generation of my Proportioners is currently available for purchase at:

www.scott.training

Cells

Cellular machinery is amazingly complex and geometric. I suggest taking 9 minutes and watching Drew Berry's 2011 Ted talk,[6] which he illustrated using his amazing scientifically-accurate 3D animations of cellular machinery—to get a feeling for the microcosm of cells.

Proteins are largely what all cellular machinery is made of. Proteins are formed from polymer chains composed of linear sequences of tens to thousands of 20 amino acid monomers. To be able to successfully perform any biological function at all, polymers must first fold into specific 3D geometries that we think of as proteins.

Predicting how amino acid sequences will fold into proteins turns out to be an extremely difficult computational problem that is the holy grail of designing drugs and vaccines. Proteins have primary, secondary, tertiary and sometimes quaternary structures all interacting to ultimately determine their 3D forms. The folding of proteins is driven by complex interactions between hydrogen and ionic bonds, Van der Waals forces, and crucially important hydrophobic forces from surrounding water molecules.

Predicting how linear amino acid chains fold into 3D proteins is known as Levinthal's paradox (1969), who noted that because of the large number of degrees of freedom in the polymer chain, a typical protein has on the order of 10^{300} possible shapes. Just to put this number in perspective, there are only 10^{81} atoms in the universe! If a single protein folded through each possibility sequentially, taking only a millionth of a second for each cycle, it should take far longer than the age of the universe to arrive at its correct shape. This is the paradox.

---

[6] https://bit.ly/3wavDey

However, we know that proteins do fold into their specific geometries perfectly in millionths of a second, millions of times every second in each cell. How this happens is not understood.

Recently DeepMind's Alpha Fold 2 neural net artificial intelligence system has made outstanding progress on a computational sub-problem of protein folding, but the problem is extremely far from being solved in general.[7]

Mammalian cells each have on the order of 10^{10} proteins. One of the most complex machines that humans build, the Airbus A350 has 2.5 million parts, some 10,000 times fewer parts than a single mammalian cell. Please keep in mind that the A350 is built by thousands of humans and it cannot divide in two and reproduce itself!

I suggest that visible cells interact with corresponding invisible minds, folding proteins as needed, for example. There is nothing qualitatively different to the relationship our brains have with our minds, only the scales are different. The principle of recursive dissociation works within minds at all scales.

Materialists tend to believe that the code of DNA must ultimately deterministically encode everything about biology—even if we do not understand all the mechanisms yet—because DNA clearly holds the information inherited by each organism. Yet, the microscopic freshwater crustacean *Daphnia pulex* has more genes than humans.[8] The largest genome we have discovered so far is the single celled *Amoeba dubia*, having 200 times more base pairs than humans (called the C-value paradox).[9] There must be more to the story than DNA explains.

---

[7] https://bit.ly/3sDwjXK

[8] https://bit.ly/39vjNly

[9] https://bit.ly/39uMqPY

While I take no issue with inheritance and the protein-coding information that DNA passes down, it is not clear how DNA determines what cells do, one level of abstraction higher than coding proteins.

Every cell in your body has the exact same DNA. How does a cell in your brain "know" to become a neuron, versus how a cell on the surface of your big toe "know" how to become a skin cell when it is assumed cells are not conscious? Biologists currently point to deterministic cell signaling and epigenetic mechanisms to explain how cells initially differentiate, hot areas for research in the last two decades. Harder still is explaining how cells maintain their differentiated identities over the course of a human lifetime—some 10^{15} cell divisions later—when neighboring cells can have entirely different structures and functions, while every cell in the body always has the exact same DNA.

It seems incredibly improbable that such complexity could be managed by a deterministic code without the fine-tuning capacity of conscious minds guiding every step of the process. It may be that the lifetime of any single cell is far less probable than the universe springing into existence with 32 dimensionless constants all randomly finely tuned to support such life. To explain away the improbability, materialists may need a multiverse for each cell, but then how would all those cellular multiverses synchronize to produce a living human composed of on the order of 10^{12} cells? The human body's total number of proteins is roughly on par with the number of stars in the universe! We are at the center of staggering complexity in the macrocosm without, and the microcosm within.

Atoms

Atoms are visible structures comprised entirely from math that is intelligible to the human mind, or at least to those of us who make the cognitive effort to understand the math and the equations. This math describes the purely geometric forms of probability density, aka atomic orbitals of electrons orbiting the nucleus. This diagram shows the geometries of the simplest element, hydrogen.

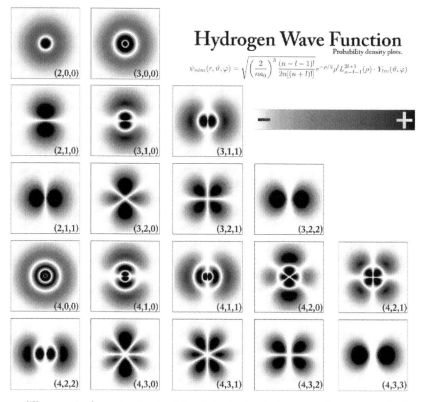

The quantized atomic orbitals of the simplest atom hydrogen at discrete energy levels.

Each orbital is characterized by precisely three quantum numbers, reminding us of other unified trinities. Varying these three quantum numbers gives rise to all the orbitals and elements in the periodic table.

Atoms are at the heart of materialism, a philosophy dating back to Democritus (460-370 BC), who has been called the "father of modern science." His atomic theory of the universe proposed:

- Everything is made of atoms.
- Atoms are indestructible and indivisible.
- Atoms are unlimited in number.
- Absolute void exists in between atoms.
- Atoms have always been and will always be in motion.

Matter and energy are only 5% of the total universe if we go with the standard model's unfalsifiable ideas of dark matter and dark energy. If we ignore these, the theory of gravity does not explain astronomical observations. Setting aside the problems with the theory of gravity and its dark fixes, it does look like the visible universe is made of atoms.

However, what does it mean to be made entirely of "ultimates" comprised of math—is not this an admission that everything is made purely of ideas? Humans can understand the math and geometry from which atoms are made. These ideas are intelligible.

Where there is matter, there is geometry.

Johannes Kepler (1571-1630) was a mathematician, astronomer, and astrologer.

Atoms are not indestructible. Einstein's famous equation $E=mc^2$ shows that matter and energy are equivalent, related only by the speed of light, squared.

Atoms can fuse together (nuclear fusion) releasing the same energy that powers stars. Atoms can radioactively decay, releasing the energy that heats planets from within, or split apart (nuclear fission) creating some terrible weapons and questionable fuel sources.

Atoms are not unlimited in number because the Big Bang created a large number, but still a finite amount, estimated at 10^{81} atoms.

Atoms are separated by a seemingly empty void, but this is permeated by virtual particles which mediate all the forces of the universe such as gravity, which acts on atoms at distances great and small.

The only bullet point in Democritus' atomic theory that holds up is that atoms have always been and will always be in motion. Hydrogen atoms created in the Big Bang are still around or have fused with other atoms to create the heavier elements, with electrons still orbiting their nuclei 13.8 billion years later.

Atom smashers (particle accelerators) were first built in the 20th century. Since then, high energy experiments show that atoms are divisible into bizarre particles called quarks which cannot exist for long outside atoms.

Quarks

Quarks are never found in isolation but only inside the atomic nucleus. Amazingly, the size of Hydrogen's nucleus (a single proton) is 5 orders of magnitude smaller than its electron orbital. If you were to enlarge the proton to the size of the Sun, the orbiting electron would be in the region of Neptune and Pluto. There is symmetry in the proportions of the simplest atom and our solar system!

Every neutron and proton contain 6 flavors of quarks: up, down, top, bottom, charm, and strange. All flavors are constantly changing into one another, but there will always be a combination of exactly 3 up / down quarks, which carry charge. The other 4 flavors can only be detected only for fleeting instants (10^{-23} seconds) when smashing nuclei apart in high energy particle collisions.

The charge of the up quark is +2/3 and the down quark carries a charge of -1/3. Each neutron has net zero charge because the up quark's +2/3 charge cancels out its two down quarks' charge of -2/3.

The proton's +1 charge comes from its two up quarks adding up to +4/3 charge plus the down quark's -1/3 charge nets out to +1. The electron's -1 charge balances the overall charge of Hydrogen's proton of +1. An interesting pattern emerges when you express the fractions as repeating decimals in base 10.

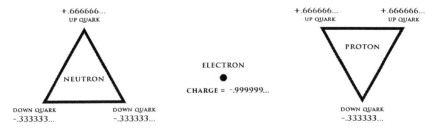

The charges of up and down quarks are what enables atoms to attract electrons.

The down quark's -1/3 charge = -.333333...
The up quark's +2/3 charge = .666666...
The electron's net -1 charge = -.999999...

I intuit that this is precisely what Tesla was talking about.

If you only knew the magnificence of the 3, 6, and 9, then you would have the key to the universe.

Nicola Tesla (1856-1843) was an inventor best known for AC electricity.

These repeating decimals can also be expressed as ninths: -3/9, +6/9, and -9/9. There are only 9 numbers in base 10, with 0 being the symbol for placeholder. Using ninths makes sense when comparing the essential relationships numbers have with each other in base 10. Another way of revealing this essence or quality is through *modular arithmetic*, the system of "wrapping around" when reaching a certain limit, instead of using a placeholder. In base 10, the limit (aka the modulo) is the value of the base's highest number, which is 9.

Modulo 9 arithmetic is quite simple. Another way of thinking about it is by adding the digits together in a multidigit number and repeating this process with each intermediate result until you end up with just one digit. The qualitative essence of the larger number is revealed when it wraps around, and the placeholder is removed.

For example, take the number 34. If you add the digits in its two places, you get 3+4=7. The essence of 34 is 7, or 34(mod 9) = 7.

In another example, take the number 55. If you add the digits in its two places, you get 5+5=10. This gives us an intermediate result because we end up with another two-digit number. We must apply the same process again, so 1+0=1. The essence of 55(mod 9) = 1.

The Fibonacci sequence is such that each number is the sum of the two preceding ones. For example, if we start with 1 and 1, then the next term in the sequence is 1+1=2. Then the next is 2+1=3, and the next is 2+3=5, and so on.

Fibonacci sequence: 1, 1, 2, 3, 5, 8, 13, 21, 34, 55, 89, 144, ...

An essential property of the Fibonacci sequence emerges through modulo 9 arithmetic, but please bear with me as I explain.

Mod 9 Fibonacci sequence: 1, 1, 2, 3, 5, 8, 4, 3, 7, 1, 8, 9, ...

If you write the sequence out in the cells of a spreadsheet you will see that the modular 9 arithmetic of the Fibonacci sequence repeats every 24 terms. Plotting these 24 essential numbers around a circle reveals remarkable patterns.

Two triangles pointing up and down each have the numbers 3, 6, and 9 on their points. All opposite numbers (180 degrees across from one another) reduce to 9. This unexpected essential symmetry in the Fibonacci sequence resonates with the charges of up and down quarks within all atoms.

The mod 9 digits of the Fibonacci sequence are plotted around the circumference, revealing two triangles, one up and one down whose vertices each connect 3,6, and 9. Art by the author.

The Fibonacci sequence is strongly correlated with the golden ratio. Dividing any two adjacent terms in the sequence approximates the golden ratio. For example, 34/21 ≈ 1.6190, 55/34 ≈ 1.6176 while the golden ratio ≈ 1.6180.

The higher the terms in the sequence, the closer the approximation will be to the golden ratio, with each pair alternating between being higher and then lower than the golden ratio, always getting closer but never actually getting there.

The Fibonacci sequence is the visible representation of an intelligible idea. Sunflowers have seeds arrayed in Fibonacci spirals that approximate the golden spiral, but the visible domain is entirely built from discrete quantized units (you do not see fractional seeds for example, but the ultimate discrete unit of the visible is the atom). If you count the sunflower seed spirals in a consistent manner you will always find a Fibonacci number.[10]

The Fibonacci sequence is not the only sequence that has a relationship with the golden ratio. You can create Fibonacci-like sequences by starting with any two numbers. For example, let us try starting out with +13 and -7. All Fibonacci-like sequences are such that each number is the sum of the two preceding ones. As you can see below, the ratios between consecutive terms quickly converge on the golden ratio, and this is true no matter which two terms form the initial conditions of the sequence that ensues.

---

[10] https://bit.ly/31BvmU4

	A	B	C
1	**Terms**	**Ratios**	**Formulas**
2		13 Arbitrary first term	
3		-7 Arbitrary second term	
4	6	-0.8571429	=A4/A3
5	-1	-0.1666667	=A5/A4
6	5	-5.0000000	=A6/A5
7	4	0.8000000	=A7/A6
8	9	2.2500000	=A8/A7
9	13	1.4444444	=A9/A8
10	22	1.6923077	=A10/A9
11	35	1.5909091	=A11/A10
12	57	1.6285714	=A12/A11
13	92	1.6140351	=A13/A12
14	149	1.6195652	=A14/A13
15	241	1.6174497	=A15/A14
16	390	1.6182573	=A16/A15
17	631	1.6179487	=A17/A16
18	1021	1.6180666	=A18/A17
19	1652	1.6180215	=A19/A18
20	2673	1.6180387	=A20/A19
21	4325	1.6180322	=A21/A20
22	6998	1.6180347	=A22/A21
23	11323	1.6180337	=A23/A22
24	18321	1.6180341	=A24/A23
25	29644	1.6180340	=A25/A24
26			
27	Golden ratio	1.6180340	

Fibonacci-like sequences can be generated from any two numbers.

The Fibonacci sequence is not something unique, but an infinite number of Fibonacci-like sequences emerge from any two initial numbers, always following the simple rule that each number in the sequence is the sum of the two preceding ones. Fibonacci-like sequences expose the fundamental relationship the golden ratio has with number. The intelligible idea from which all discrete Fibonacci-like sequences derive is the golden ratio.

Deep numerical connections exist between the triangular array of atomic electron configurations (organized into s, p, d, and f shells), the triangular array of electron shells and subshells, and Pascal's triangle (triangular array of binomial coefficients arising in algebra, combinatorics, and probability theory). The diagonal rule in electron shells yields the filling sequence, while the diagonal rule in Pascal's triangle yields the Fibonacci sequence. These are symmetric.

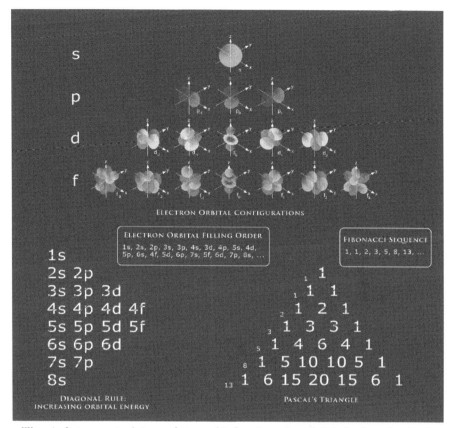

There is deep symmetry between electron orbital configurations and shells, Pascal's triangle, orbital filling sequence, and the Fibonacci sequence. Upper image: Haade CC BY-SA 3.0

The golden ratio is the key to universal physics.

Sir Edward Appleton, (1892-1965) received the Nobel Prize in physics in 1947.

If subatomic structure is entirely quantized & mathematical, then so too is everything made with atoms (the universe). Saying that everything is made of mathematics is like saying everything is made of Latin. Yes, the universe is mathematical—but math (& Latin) are relationships invented by and understood only by consciousness.

8 | Questions and Answers

Having a new way of thinking sink in is a process which takes time and reflection. To help you kick it off, I recommend reading through the following Top 10 list, even if you feel like you already know the answers to most of these questions.

We believe what we see and then we believe our interpretation of it, we don't even know we are making an interpretation most of the time. We think this is reality.

Robert Anton Wilson (1932-2007) was an author and "agnostic mystic."

Bernardo Kastrup has blazed the trail of the philosophy of modern idealism[1] and addressed many common objections to this worldview. Some of my Top 10 were inspired by his clear thinking.

1. **If everything is imaginary, why does hitting my thumb with a hammer hurt?**

    Experiencing pain, solidity, or ineffable suchness are real qualities of experience (qualia). The pain you experience is real because you are conscious of it. A "real" hammer outside consciousness is an abstraction, a subliminal artifact of the standard explanatory model.

---

[1] Kastrup, B. (2019). The Idea of the World: A Multi-Disciplinary Argument for the Mental Nature of Reality.

2. **Why do we experience separate minds if there is "one universal mind," or if "all is consciousness?"**

    We experience private minds because of the phenomenon of dissociation, which can be studied in microcosm in the mental health dissociative identity disorder (formerly called multiple personality disorder).

    In a larger sense, separate individuals' minds are dissociated identities within the same super-mind, integral to the consciousness that informs them as alters.

3. **Does consciousness survive death?**

    The standard worldview says that your consciousness ends when your brain dies, period. Brain death is used as an indicator of legal death. However, consciousness is the only reality, transcending bodies, brains, even space and time. Consciousness cannot ever die.

    Invisible minds appear to survive the visible death of brains and bodies. Near death experiences reveal rich invisible phenomenology occurring simultaneously with no visible brain activity.[2]

    Talented mediums can communicate with souls of the deceased. What they do is real.[3]

    Many religions are based on the belief that when your body dies your soul does not. They are correct based on subjective medium communication, but this cannot be verified by science because the soul cannot be weighed and measured in the visible domain.

---

[2] Alexander, Eben (2012) Proof of Heaven: A Neurosurgeon's Journey into the Afterlife

[3] Marie Manuchehri specializes in clairvoyance, clairaudience, and medium communication. She is amazing and her website is www.energyintuitive.com

Science cannot accept anything beyond world mind based on its historical definition as split from religion, whose purview extends beyond the visible domain. I believe we discarded too much, and science would be fuller if allowed to investigate realms beyond the visible.

4. Does the world continue to exist when I am not observing it?

You experience a mind interacting within a vast hierarchy of other minds. When you close your eyes or sleep, world mind remains aware of its contents. Sleeping or sticking your head in the sand does not make the world disappear.

If a tree falls in a forest and no one is around to hear it, does it make a sound?

Classic statement inspired by the immaterialism of George Berkeley, but he never wrote it like that. It was put in this form in the 20th century.

The answer to the question is yes because world and soul minds are always around to hear it, even when your individual body and soul are not present in the forest.

5. If all is mental, then why is the universe so orderly? My mind is certainly not like that.

Consciousness does not necessarily have to behave in the chaotic way the human mind flits between thoughts, emotions, distractions, beliefs, waking, sleep, dreams, forgetfulness, intoxication, mental disorders, and so on.

The anthropomorphized "laws of nature" might be better expressed as conscious decisions, which were made by super-minds fine-tuning the universe to support more sub-minds. These decisions may possibly change in time to better support complexity.

Perhaps one day dark energy will reverse its polarity and galaxies will start accelerating back toward one another, destined to ultimately implode back into singular point of nothingness in a Big Crunch. Symmetry and the beautiful order of the visible universe suggests this possibility: breathe out, breathe in, repeat.

6. **Is the universe merely a figment of my imagination?**

No, because idealism is not solipsism. The solipsist assumes that all people and the world are in their mind. They assume no phenomena exist outside their individual mind.

Idealism assumes people are conscious—real sources of experiences. World mind is independent of their individual dissociated mind.

Universal mind is also not solipsistic because awareness transcends it and all sub-minds. The universe is not a solipsistic mind of God.

7. **How come we cannot simply imagine a better world and immediately wish it into being?**

Consider dreams, hallucinations, obsessive/compulsive thoughts, or emotions that our egos do not identify with, yet are nevertheless experienced in our individual minds. Many aspects of our psyches are beyond the control of ego and will.

Individual ego is a tiny ship within the great ocean of dissociated minds swimming in awareness. The wishes of ego and the power of its will are limited.

Your imagination is bounded within your individual mind. Your ideas are not shared with other minds unless you act to make your ideas cross dissociative boundaries. If you want to manifest a better world consider writing a book, making a video, doing a podcast, lecturing, inventing something new, and so on.

Creating by working within the boundaries of transpersonal archetypes is a powerful strategy in many creative endeavors because our psyches all have access to the mind of our collective human soul.

Fiction, politics, and belief systems tend to be built leveraging the power of archetypes, which we all immediately understand.

A mythological image that has to be explained to the brain is not working.

Joseph Campbell (1904-1987) described the journey of the archetypal hero spanning world myths in his book The Hero with a Thousand Faces.

Tech advances tend to be built by first understanding the rules that structure world mind. Invention is creativity constrained by and working within the boundaries of world mind (aka the laws of physics) to manifest new models.

You never change things by fighting the existing reality. To change something, build a new model that makes the existing model obsolete.

Buckminster Fuller (1895-1983) was a free thinker, architect, inventor, and author of more than 30 books.

---

8. **How can the universe exist in consciousness if consciousness arose billions of years after the Big Bang?**

This question assumes that consciousness arises only in animal biology, which is part of the standard materialist storyline. The alternative worldview proposed in this book suggests that consciousness existed prior to the Big Bang and that the inanimate universe and much later the emergence of animate life within it are interacting relative dissociations of universal mind, which are themselves modulations of absolute consciousness.

9. **If consciousness is not generated by the brain, how come probing the brain correlates strongly with inner experience?**

Probing an open brain in surgery and hearing the subject describe their inner experience when specific areas are stimulated is how brain function was initially mapped. The question assumes that this probing proves that consciousness arises in the brain, reinforcing the materialist belief.

An analogy is helpful here in clarifying the situation. Imagine that the brain is a TV that tunes into a person's favorite series which is being streamed from the Netflix of their mind. Probing the TV's semiconductors is bound to cause interference with the show, and may alter its colors, compression artifacts, buffering, and qualities of reception. Fooling around with the visible hardware *does not prove that the show* is *inside the TV*, just that the TV and the invisible series are strongly correlated in experience.

Studying this objective-subjective boundary is an interesting area which can teach us about the relationship between the visible brain and invisible mind. Manipulating the brain through surgery or dissociative drugs affects the body-soul interface.

However, if the boundary is opened too far, a person loses their sense of self, which commonly happens with dissociative drugs such as LSD, DMT, etc. This can be liberating and terrifying, depending on how strongly one identifies with the limitations of the boundary of individual self.

Project MK Ultra was a program of experiments on human subjects undertaken by the US Central Intelligence Agency from 1953-73. The BBC TV mini-series documentary, "Can't Get You Out of My Head" (2021) delved into this program and profiled cases where the subjects were treated with psychoactive drugs, electroshocks, hypnosis, sensory deprivation, isolation, sexual abuse, and other forms of torture—all without consent—in an illegal attempt to learn how to destroy and control human minds for nefarious purposes.

The program failed in many of its specific goals but succeeded in killing people and destroying minds such that some subjects survived with no memories of their previous lives or understanding of how to navigate the complex cultural and social contexts in which they continued to live. It was as if their TVs changed channels and displayed new shows.

I speculate that MK Ultra's program decoupled the original souls from their corresponding bodies and then new souls informed after the subject's bodies recovered. This would explain why subjects had no ability to recall any details of their former lives—it was as if they were newly born. Clearly MK Ultra was a heinous crime that should never be repeated.

We do not fully understand the interdependency between bodies & souls. There are ethical, consensual ways to gently probe the objective-subjective boundary—there is no need to go medieval on people to transcend the individual self.

10. Is there more to consciousness than being an individual person?

All we know is experience but there is no independent 'we' or 'I' that knows experience. There is just experience or experiencing. And experiencing is not inherently divided into one part that experiences and another part that is experienced.

Rupert Spira (1960-) is a teacher of non-dual consciousness.

"Enlightenment" is exactly what Spira described above, realizing there is no "I" character which knows experience. There is only the experiencing of our shared being.[4]

---

[4] https://bit.ly/3dgh1BQ

9 | Transformation

The sacredness of geometry can transform you. By experiencing it yourself, you can reconnect with transpersonal, transcendental qualities of truth, beauty, and bliss.

Problems with Business as Usual

The dominant global paradigm defines society's assumptions about the nature of reality and the individual's place in it, whether we are cognizant of it or not.

Science and religion separated during the European Enlightenment and this separation allowed us to see everything non-material as a matter of belief, and everything material as resources to study and engineer for human benefit. Humanity has reaped untold benefits from looking at the world as materials to be exploited and our population exploded.

However, in the 21st century we are increasingly realizing the dominant paradigm and its largely unexamined philosophy of scientific materialism is literally undermining the world for human habitation. This has left us with a sense of futility and exposed the meaninglessness of our achievements in the face of anthropogenic pollution and climate change with consequent unprecedented increase in the frequency of environmental disasters. What use was engineering the world for human benefit if we end up making the planet uninhabitable for our species?

There must be something deeply wrong with our assumptions about the nature of reality and our hubris in exploiting nature. We desperately need a new way of thinking.

Relative and Absolute Truths

Recently, global politics have become disconnected from facts and truths that we used to hold in common and perceive as self-evident. As more and more gets politicized we undermine the notion of truth itself and democratic governance will possibly soon become untenable.

We urgently need to consider the possibility that there may be some forms of truth which are universal and not relative to groups or individuals.

The shared consensual reality of hurricanes, frozen regions not accustomed to arctic temperatures, megafires, or death of millions through viral infection is teaching us the hard way that universal truth does exist, at least in the natural world.

What else beside the natural world is universally true? Religious beliefs vary widely. Cultural beliefs vary widely. Political beliefs vary widely. Opinion varies widely. Scientific opinion varies widely. The language of mathematics including its most accessible branch—geometry is universally true.

You can't criticize geometry. It's never wrong.

Paul Rand (1914-1996) was a graphic designer best known for his many globally recognized corporate logos.

By establishing a personal practice with geometry, you can connect with this form of universal truth. This practice can be meaningful, beautiful, feel good, and many even report a sense of sacredness or preciousness to the experience that is unique and free of the baggage of traditional beliefs.

Working with qualitative geometry can also stimulate the innate creativity & curiosity we all once had as children, and you might enjoy connection with others sharing in this transformative experience.

Working with quantitative geometry can help develop and strengthen your powers of logic and rationality and can also possibly directly improve your skills if you work in a field which uses drawings or 3D models.

Paying Attention

If you are old enough, do you remember your mind not being so fragmented in the 1990s as it has become recently? It might not just be the ageing process. Current mobile information technology has most user's minds feeling fragmented. Studies show that attention spans have been decreasing since 2000 and presently are less than the notoriously distracted goldfish.[1] Congratulations if you have made it this far through the book!

The complete hollowing out of attention has been driven by algorithms and advertisements insidiously designed by teams of specialists to capture our attention with short articles and clickbait.

Setting aside a time and place to disconnect from electronic distraction and actively practice mental focus is increasingly important for mental health. Sacred geometry practice is perfect for strengthening focus because it keeps both hemispheres of your brain engaged, and this can help keep you from becoming distracted.

A sacred geometry practice using the traditional instruments of paper, pencil, ruler & compass is an antidote to electronification and is an elegant anachronism not to be missed. If you go this route, I recommend that you turn off your phone entirely if possible.

---

[1] https://bit.ly/3ftVEzF

An iPad Pro with Apple Pencil or Microsoft Surface with Surface Pen have certain advantages over the traditional instruments (not least of which they are more accurate and flexible), yet the digital approach is disadvantaged by comparison in some other ways.

Phones screens are too small to be adequate for drawing and drawing with the tips of your fingers is not accurate enough. I recommend everyone start out with the traditional instruments. The traditional approach is a fine one that never has to end.

You might possibly grow into a digital approach if it interests you, you can afford the right equipment, you find the process intuitive, and you are able to avoid digital distraction.

Quest for Meaning

The fact that the entire universe is minded, purposeful, and therefore intrinsically **meaningful** should bring tremendous relief, having suffered as we have for so long under a misguided dominant paradigm, which pathologically trivializes and even denies the very existence of meaning in lieu of big data & operant conditioning.

Realizing that there is only one consciousness, means separation is only a stubbornly persistent illusion of our dissociated minds. We are always experiencing awareness through all our partitioned alters together.

Truth, beauty, and goodness are transcendent virtues everyone recognizes but which a dying, cynical culture seeks to deny. Striving to manifest the transcendentals in the mundane can give life meaning that you may have been looking for.

Applying creativity to harmonize your personal microcosm with the universal macrocosm is its own meaningful reward.

A group mandala in the process of being created at one of my past residential workshops.

Geometry is a Vehicle

Using the qualitative aspect of geometry to experience the intelligible is an express elevator to the top floor of universal mind. Arriving on the top intelligible floor is a clear signal of your intention to interact with your higher soul healers (aka higher selves). Many are deeply affected by experiencing the sacredness of geometry in ways that are difficult to articulate.

While geometry occupies your mind with the qualities of the universal language, the qualia of awareness shines forth, and you begin to apprehend the ineffable suchness behind the forms and of life in general. The particulars of geometry then do not matter, for geometry ultimately is only a vehicle that can take you from mundane point A to sacred point B.

The proposed alternative worldview is not something to believe in, but to analyze and contemplate in your own experience. Only then will you know if you prefer its vantage to the standard worldview.

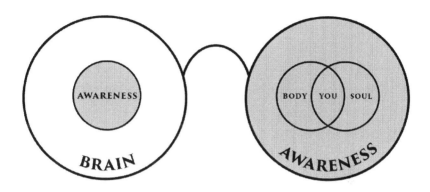

You see it now, congratulations! That is an important step at the beginning of any hero's journey.

A journey of a thousand miles begins with a single step.

Lao Tzu (6th century BC – 4th century BC) whose name means "old master" was a semi-legendary philosopher who purportedly wrote the Tao Te Ching.

The next step is to experience the sacredness of geometry by enrolling and/or subscribing at:

sacredgeometryacademy.com

About the Author

Scott Onstott was born and raised in California and received his Bachelor of Arts degree in Architecture from the University of California in 1992.

Scott is the author of dozens of books, has taught over a thousand students face-to-face, and his numerous courses have millions of views worldwide. His professional experience includes architectural and product design, computer aided design, polygonal & solid 3d modelling, rendering, real-time simulation, C# programming, digital art, vector illustration, motion graphics, and character animation.

Scott emigrated to British Columbia in 2004, where he resides with his wife and son. Scott is a dual US/Canadian citizen.

The author was born missing three limbs and does not identify as a victim, but rather appreciates his unique physical limitations for teaching him important lessons early in life.

Made in the USA
Middletown, DE
25 June 2021